DEMANDING ACCOUNTABILITY: THE ADMINISTRATION'S RECKLESS RELEASE OF TERRORISTS FROM GUANTANAMO

HEARING

BEFORE THE

COMMITTEE ON FOREIGN AFFAIRS
HOUSE OF REPRESENTATIVES

ONE HUNDRED FOURTEENTH CONGRESS

SECOND SESSION

JULY 7, 2016

Serial No. 114–203

Printed for the use of the Committee on Foreign Affairs

Available via the World Wide Web: http://www.foreignaffairs.house.gov/ or
http://www.gpo.gov/fdsys/

U.S. GOVERNMENT PUBLISHING OFFICE

20–652PDF   WASHINGTON : 2016

For sale by the Superintendent of Documents, U.S. Government Publishing Office
Internet: bookstore.gpo.gov   Phone: toll free (866) 512–1800; DC area (202) 512–1800
Fax: (202) 512–2104   Mail: Stop IDCC, Washington, DC 20402–0001

COMMITTEE ON FOREIGN AFFAIRS

EDWARD R. ROYCE, California, *Chairman*

CHRISTOPHER H. SMITH, New Jersey
ILEANA ROS-LEHTINEN, Florida
DANA ROHRABACHER, California
STEVE CHABOT, Ohio
JOE WILSON, South Carolina
MICHAEL T. McCAUL, Texas
TED POE, Texas
MATT SALMON, Arizona
DARRELL E. ISSA, California
TOM MARINO, Pennsylvania
JEFF DUNCAN, South Carolina
MO BROOKS, Alabama
PAUL COOK, California
RANDY K. WEBER SR., Texas
SCOTT PERRY, Pennsylvania
RON DeSANTIS, Florida
MARK MEADOWS, North Carolina
TED S. YOHO, Florida
CURT CLAWSON, Florida
SCOTT DesJARLAIS, Tennessee
REID J. RIBBLE, Wisconsin
DAVID A. TROTT, Michigan
LEE M. ZELDIN, New York
DANIEL DONOVAN, New York

ELIOT L. ENGEL, New York
BRAD SHERMAN, California
GREGORY W. MEEKS, New York
ALBIO SIRES, New Jersey
GERALD E. CONNOLLY, Virginia
THEODORE E. DEUTCH, Florida
BRIAN HIGGINS, New York
KAREN BASS, California
WILLIAM KEATING, Massachusetts
DAVID CICILLINE, Rhode Island
ALAN GRAYSON, Florida
AMI BERA, California
ALAN S. LOWENTHAL, California
GRACE MENG, New York
LOIS FRANKEL, Florida
TULSI GABBARD, Hawaii
JOAQUIN CASTRO, Texas
ROBIN L. KELLY, Illinois
BRENDAN F. BOYLE, Pennsylvania

AMY PORTER, *Chief of Staff*   THOMAS SHEEHY, *Staff Director*
JASON STEINBAUM, *Democratic Staff Director*

CONTENTS

DEMANDING ACCOUNTABILITY: THE ADMINISTRATION'S RECKLESS RELEASE OF TERRORISTS FROM GUANTANAMO

THURSDAY, JULY 7, 2016

HOUSE OF REPRESENTATIVES,
COMMITTEE ON FOREIGN AFFAIRS,
Washington, DC.

The committee met, pursuant to notice, at 10 o'clock a.m., in room 2172 Rayburn House Office Building, Hon. Edward Royce (chairman of the committee) presiding.

Chairman ROYCE. This hearing will come to order.

Today we welcome back the Obama administration's top officials for closing the detention center at Guantanamo Bay. In March, these two gentlemen appeared before the committee to discuss the administration's proposal to relocate the prison and its detainees to the continental United States, as well as the process of releasing individuals to foreign countries.

Much of the news from that hearing surrounded Mr. Lewis' revelation that, in his words, "unfortunately, there have been Americans that have died because of Guantanamo detainees." And, indeed, last month the Washington Post reported that the administration believes that at least 12 detainees released from the Guantanamo facility have since attacked U.S. or allied forces in Afghanistan, killing about a half dozen Americans.

That was startling enough. But it is particularly disturbing that—upon close examination—these witnesses made statements to the committee that are inconsistent with the documents and inconsistent with information that the administration has supplied the committee under the law.

Specifically, the committee asked whether the Department of Defense ever knowingly transferred a detainee to a country that did not exhibit an ability to substantially mitigate the risk of recidivism or maintain custody or control of that individual. Mr. Lewis and Mr. Wolosky assured committee members that it had not. Yet numerous intelligence reports provided by the administration suggest that their answers were inaccurate: In fact, the Defense Department had done so on numerous occasions.

The Secretary of State has the sole responsibility to negotiate transfers, including agreements to monitor released detainees. Under the law, Congress regularly receives information from the intelligence community on the return to terrorism rate of individ-

(1)

uals released to foreign countries as well as assessments of a country's ability to prevent terrorists from returning to the fight.

Simply put, many countries just aren't up to the job. And a diplomatic agreement to do the job isn't worth the paper it is written on if a country does not have the resources, does not have the training to keep committed terrorists from returning to the battlefield.

Yet the administration has sent Guantanamo terrorists to these countries anyway. To then deceive this committee and the American people is deeply disturbing, and when given the opportunity to correct the record for the committee, they ignored us.

I appreciate that the administration finally responded on Tuesday. But it shouldn't take the calling of a hearing to elicit a return letter, especially on something as consequential as this. This committee has an obligation to conduct oversight. While we have differences of opinion over Guantanamo policy, I don't think anyone here finds the administration's dismissiveness acceptable.

And should anyone think the committee's concerns are theoretical, and specifically I was pressing on these terrorists who had been transferred to Uruguay, it is not theoretical because now Jihad Diyab, who is an al-Qaeda-linked terrorist, was sent from Guantanamo to Uruguay in December 2014.

We sounded the alarm about Uruguay's lack of legal framework. We explained to you about the critical resources to prevent travel outside the country—that that was lacking in the case of Uruguay. And so what is the result?

The result is last month, Jihad Diyab disappeared from Uruguay. His current whereabouts are unknown, and this was after Mr. Wolosky testified to us in March that "we are confident that the Government of Uruguay is taking appropriate steps to substantially mitigate the risk" of this former detainee and others sent to Uruguay. Yesterday, CNN, citing U.S. officials, reported that this terrorist was last spotted in Venezuela. He is believed to be headed back to Syria or Yemen.

We have been awaiting answers to the committee's inquiry. But while I've been patient, the President has been in a rush, seemingly willing to release Guantanamo terrorists to wherever he can.

I wish we were not here today. Holding another Guantanamo hearing this week was not my intention. But he is loose and my patience has run out.

And I now turn to the ranking member.

Mr. ENGEL. Thank you, Mr. Chairman, and Mr. Wolosky and Mr. Lewis, welcome back and thank you for your service.

Last time you gentlemen were here I made my views on the Guantanamo Prison pretty clear and I would ask that my opening statement from that hearing be included as part of the record of this hearing.

Chairman ROYCE. Without objection.

Mr. ENGEL. To recap, the prison should be closed. National security experts of both parties agree with me. In fact, I have a letter here from 36 retired generals and admirals calling for the prison's closure and I ask that it be included in the record.

The prison is a waste of money and a propaganda tool for terrorists. End of story, as far as the prison goes. There were, however, some issues raised about transferred detainees at the last hearing that deserve some follow up and I say transferred rather than released because there's an extensive process that goes into removing a detainee from the prison and sending him to another country.

It's not as though they are just set loose. But it is important to know how exactly are we monitoring transferred detainees and assessing the risk they pose. Those are good questions.

But because they deal with intelligence methods we can only discuss them in a closed classified setting. My understanding is that the administration offered to do just that and that offer was rebuffed.

I hope that after this hearing in a few weeks or so we can have a closed classified setting to get answers to some questions that you are not really allowed to say here in open session.

So why are we here? The title of today's hearing is demanding accountability of the administration's reckless release of terrorists from Guantanamo.

Since we say reckless release, it sounds like people's minds are made up and I want to make sure all the facts are on the table because I think there's plenty of blame to go all around. I think the chairman raises legitimate issues but I do think there's plenty of blame to go around.

First, the vast majority of Guantanamo detainees were transferred out of the prison before President Obama took office. A total of 780 detainees have been held in Guantanamo.

During the Bush administration, 500 were transferred out, compared to 159 detainees under President Obama. Secondly, let's look at the number of transferred detainees who returned to the battlefield. The figure 30 percent gets thrown around a lot but what goes into that number?

Turns out it includes the total number of transferred detainees that we know for sure have returned to the fight as well as those suspected of re-engagement over the entire life of the Guantanamo Prison 2001 to present.

During the Bush years, 2001 to 2008, the rate of suspected and confirmed cases of re-engagement was actually higher than that, 35 percent, with 21 percent of the cases confirmed and 14 percent suspected.

So let me say that again. More than one-third of the terrorists that President Bush's administration transferred may have returned to the fight. Now let's contrast that with the Obama administration.

Under President Obama, that number, again, totaling suspected and confirmed cases, drops to 13 percent. Eight percent suspected and just 5 percent confirmed. That 5 percent represents seven people.

Now, I know one person escaping this is one person too much. But I just want to have a balanced hearing here because if we've already made up our minds and talking about the administration being reckless, it doesn't seem to me like we are really here to learn anything more.

I reiterate at most 13 percent of those transfers since January 2009 have re-engaged compared to as much as 35 percent during the previous administration. The contrast is striking. But let's not get lost in the numbers because this is perhaps the most important point.

The transferred detainees who returned to the battlefield and killed Americans were let out during the Bush administration, not during the Obama administration.

So if we are going to paint with a broad brush and say 30 percent of transferred detainees may be going back to the fight and killing Americans, we need to take the whole story and put it into perspective. The Bush administration racked up that average and then some.

The Obama administration has helped to bring it back down. Thirdly, the administration's closure plan would not transfer any person who does not meet the most stringent criteria.

I've heard claims that the remaining detainees are the worst of the worst and the administration simply wants to turn them loose. That's false.

Twenty-nine of 79 remaining detainees are cleared for transfer. Among them are 22 Yemenis. The administration isn't transferring them yet. As a matter of policy we transfer detainees to their home countries. But in the case of Yemen the government cannot provide adequate security assurances.

So the administration has pumped the brakes out of an abundance of caution. We need to find countries that can provide adequate assurances before those 22 are transferred.

That leaves 50. Some of these are really bad guys. Ten of them will stand trial. Another 40 are being legitimately held as prisoners of war. But under no circumstances, in my opinion, is the Obama administration simply opening the gate and releasing dangerous terrorists onto the street.

Look, Guantanamo is a mess and it always has been. No one is blameless. Anyone can cherry pick single cases to paint a picture big or small, good or bad. But I think the facts and the statistics speak for themselves.

And I think what we should do after this, instead of having the witnesses come and tell us that they can only tell us things in a classified briefing, is to spend our time with them after this hearing in a few weeks where we could be in a closed setting getting to the bottom of this matter.

Now, the Foreign Affairs Committee obviously has oversight on this issue. The hearing last March and today's hearing are the only two times that the committee has taken up this issue in the nearly 15 years that Guantanamo Prison has been open. So since we have our top Guantanamo experts with us today, I hope you can give us your opinions on some interesting ideas we've recently heard about that prison. I am going to read you a few quotes.

You may recognize them. I'll give you a hint. It's one of the candidates running for President. Here's the first:

> "This morning I watched President Obama talking about Gitmo, Guantanamo Bay, which by the way we are keeping open and we are going to load it up with some bad dudes. We're going to load it up."

And the second quote:

''Torture works, okay, folks. Believe me, it works, and water boarding is your minor form. Some people say it is not actually torture. Let's assume it is. But they ask me the question, what do you think of water boarding? Absolutely fine, but we should go much stronger than waterboarding. We should go much stronger because our country is in trouble.''

So I just want to say that I read that because, you know, some people say they want to expand the Guantanamo Prison and torture. I can't think of a worse proposal for our national security. These schemes would only harm us with their allies and provide ammunition to our adversaries. Mr. Wolosky, Mr. Lewis, at some point today maybe we can hear your views on what would happen if we went in that direction.

Again, I hate doing tit for tats but I do think it is not really fair to blame the administration for all the frustrations we have about Guantanamo when we see that there were problems and wrong things done in the previous administration as well. So I look forward to listening to you and hearing your thoughts and thank you, Mr. Chairman.

Chairman ROYCE. Thank you, Mr. Engel.

This morning we are pleased to be joined by Special Envoy Lee Wolosky, Special Envoy for Guantanamo Closure at the U.S. Department of State. Previously, Mr. Wolosky served as the Director for Transnational Threats on the National Security Council under President Clinton.

And Mr. Paul Lewis is joining us. We are pleased that he is here, Special Envoy for Guantanamo Detention Closure at the U.S. Department of Defense. Previously, Mr. Lewis served as both the general counsel and the minority general counsel on the U.S. Armed Services Committee. Without objection, the witnesses' full prepared statements will be made part of the record.

Members will have 5 calendar days to submit any statements or questions or any extraneous material they might want to submit for the record and I'd like to remind everyone including our witnesses that willful misrepresentation or false statements by a witness is a criminal offense under 18 U.S. Code § 1001.

Indeed, that is the case for all of our hearings and Special Envoy Wolosky, please summarize your remarks.

STATEMENT OF MR. LEE WOLOSKY, SPECIAL ENVOY FOR GUANTANAMO CLOSURE, U.S. DEPARTMENT OF STATE

Mr. WOLOSKY. Thank you very much, Mr. Chairman, Ranking Member Engel, distinguished members of the committee. Good morning.

I appreciate your inviting me once again to appear before this committee. I look forward to continuing our discussion in closed session either later today as we have offered or as soon as possible so that we can have a fuller discussion of some of the classified topics we know are of interest to the committee.

Altogether, a total of 779 detainees have passed through Guantanamo and of those 700 have departed. The vast majority of detainees transferred out of Guantanamo to other countries—some 532— were transferred by the administration of George W. Bush. Under

President Obama, a total of 159 detainees have been transferred. Today, 79 remain.

President Bush acted to whittle the detainee population because he understood that, and I quote, ''the detention facility had become a propaganda tool for our enemies and a distraction for our allies.'' President Obama has continued detainee transfers for many of the same reasons. Of the 79 detainees detained at Guantanamo today, 29 are currently approved for transfer. Detainees have been designated as approved for transfer during this administration through one of two rigorous interagency processes.

First, soon after taking office, President Obama ordered the first ever comprehensive interagency review of all of the 242 detainees then in U.S. custody.

In 2009 and 2010, the Guantanamo Review Task Force, sometimes also called the Executive Order Task Force, which was comprised of more than 60 national security professionals from across the government, assembled all reasonable available information relevant to determining an appropriate disposition for each detainee.

Then, based on the task force's recommendations, the Departments of Defense, State, Justice and Homeland Security, the Office of the Director for National Intelligence and the Joint Chiefs of Staff unanimously determined the appropriate disposition for each detainee: Transfer, referral for prosecution or continued law of war detention.

Second, pursuant to Executive Order 13567, detainees who are not—who were not approved for transfer in 2009 and 2010 could be subject to additional review by the Periodic Review Board.

The PRB is comprised of senior representatives from six agencies and departments. None of the PRB representatives are political appointees.

Having described how Guantanamo detainees have been approved for transfer, I would now like to briefly describe the process for transferring detainees.

Decisions regarding whether, when and where to transfer a detainee are the culmination of another rigorous interagency process. The Department of State leads diplomatic negotiations with foreign governments regarding the transfer of Guantanamo detainees.

But we are typically joined in our discussions by senior career officials from the Departments of Defense, Justice and Homeland Security as well as those in the intelligence community and on the joint staff. Generally, transfer negotiations occur in two steps.

First, the U.S. Government obtains or reconfirms a political commitment that the potential receiving country is willing in principle to resettle or repatriate detainees and to impose various measures that will substantially mitigate the threat the detainees may pose after transfer.

Second, we engage in technical discussions with foreign officials responsible for implementing these measures. These technical discussions offer the opportunity to tailor the integration and security measures to specific circumstances under consideration, to share best practices from previous detainee transfers and perhaps most importantly to determine based on an individualized assessment of these specific circumstances whether the statutory standard in the

NDAA governing the foreign transfer of Guantanamo detainees can be met.

Once we conclude that our diplomatic negotiations will result in a security framework that we assess will substantially mitigate the threat a detainee may pose after transfer, the Secretary of Defense consults with the Secretaries of State, Homeland Security and the Attorney General, the Director of National Intelligence and the Chairman of the Joint Chiefs of Staff on the transfer.

Only after the Secretary of Defense receives the views of those principals and only if he is satisfied that the requirements of the NDAA are satisfied does the Secretary of Defense sign and transmit a certification to the Congress conveying his intention to transfer detainees.

Ladies and gentlemen of the committee, let me close by saying that although we would obviously prefer that no former detainees engage in terrorist or insurgent activity following his transfer, we believe that the low rate of confirmed re-engagement for detainees transferred since January 2009, under 5 percent, is testament to the rigorous interagency approach the administration has taken to both approving detainees for transfer and to negotiating and vetting detainee transfer frameworks.

I look forward to your questions.

[The prepared statement of Mr. Wolosky follows:]

Department of State
Special Envoy for Guantanamo Closure Lee S. Wolosky
Opening Statement
House Foreign Affairs Committee
Hearing on Guantanamo Bay
July 7, 2016

Introduction

Chairman Royce, Ranking Member Engel, distinguished Members of the Committee: Good morning. I appreciate you inviting me once again to appear before this Committee to discuss the important matter of closing the U.S. detention facility at Guantanamo Bay, Cuba (GTMO). I look forward to continuing our discussion in a closed session, either later today as we have offered or as soon as practicable, so that we can have a fuller, classified discussion of some of the topics we know are of interest to the Committee.

I.   Current Population & Review Process

I will begin with an overview of the current detainee population at Guantanamo and the process by which decisions are made to approve a detainee for transfer or to continue law of war detention. Today, there are 79 individuals detained at Guantanamo. No detainees have been transferred to Guantanamo since 2008. Altogether, a total of 779 detainees have passed through Guantanamo and, of those 700 have departed. The vast majority of detainees transferred out of Guantanamo to other countries—some 532—were transferred by President George W. Bush, prior to the commencement of President Obama's administration on January 20, 2009. Under President Obama, a total of 159 detainees have been transferred from Guantanamo.

President Bush acted to whittle the detainee population because he understood that "the detention facility had become a propaganda tool for our enemies and a distraction for our allies."[1] President Obama has continued detainee transfers and, as you know, signed an executive order to close Guantanamo as one of his first official acts as President.[2] Soon after taking office, President Obama also ordered the first ever comprehensive, interagency review of all the 242 detainees then in custody at Guantanamo.[3]

In 2009-2010, the Guantanamo Review Task Force (sometimes also called the Executive Order Task Force, or "EOTF"), which was composed of more than 60 national security professionals, including intelligence analysts, law enforcement officials, and attorneys, drawn from the Department of Justice, Department of Defense, Department of State, Department of Homeland Security, the Office of the Director of National Intelligence, the Central Intelligence Agency, the Federal Bureau of Investigation, and other agencies within the U.S. government, assembled all reasonably available information from across the government relevant to determining an appropriate disposition of each detainee. The review task force examined this information

---

[1] GEORGE W. BUSH, DECISION POINTS 180 (2010).

[2] E.O. 13492, January 22, 2009.

[3] E.O. 13493, January 22, 2009.

critically, giving careful consideration to the threat posed by the detainee, the reliability of the underlying information, and the interests of national security. Then, based on the review task force's recommendations, the Departments of Defense, State, Justice and Homeland Security, the Office of the Director of National Intelligence, and the Joint Chiefs of Staff unanimously determined the appropriate disposition for each detainee: transfer, referral for prosecution, or continued law-of-war detention.[4]

Pursuant to Executive Order 13567, promulgated on March 7, 2011, detainees who were not approved for transfer in 2009-2010, and who have not been charged by military commission or are not serving a sentence, are subject to additional review by the Periodic Review Board (PRB). The PRB's mandate is to determine whether a detainee's continued detention is necessary to protect against a continuing significant threat to the security of the United States. The PRB is composed of senior representatives from the Department of Defense, the Joint Chiefs of Staff, the Department of Justice, the Department of Homeland Security, the Office of the Director of National Intelligence, and the Department of State. Importantly, none of the PRB representatives are political appointees. Detainees appearing before the PRB are assigned a personal representative and have the opportunity to be represented by private counsel, at no expense to the government. Detainees can provide an oral and written statement, submit evidence, call witnesses, and elect to answer questions from Board members.

Pursuant to the EO, detainees who are designated for continued detention by the PRB receive a file review every six months and another full review and hearing every three years. If the PRB determines that there is a significant question regarding whether the detainee's continued detention is warranted in a biannual file review, the Board convenes a full review.

So far, the PRB has conducted initial hearings for 53 detainees, nine file reviews, and four subsequent full reviews. Of the 53 initial PRB hearings, 20 detainees were approved for transfer, 16 were determined to meet the standard for continued detention, and the results of 15 hearings are still pending. Of those 16 who were determined to meet the standard for continued detention, nine file reviews have been held, and five have resulted in subsequent full reviews, of which four have been conducted. Each of the four subsequent full reviews yielded a decision to approve the detainee for transfer. One full review is pending. This track record demonstrates that the PRB is neither a rubberstamp for release nor one for continued detention, and reflects the objective evaluation of the facts and circumstances attendant to each individual case.

Of the 79 detainees who remain at GTMO today, 29 are approved for transfer. Of these, 15 were approved by the 2009-2010 review task force and 14 were approved for transfer through the Periodic Review Board process.

Ten detainees are in some phase of the military commissions criminal justice process—either awaiting a trial or appeal, or serving a sentence.

The remaining 30 are currently designated for continued detention but will continue to be subject to by the PRBs.

---

[4] GUANTANAMO REVIEW TASK FORCE, FINAL REPORT i-ii (2010).

II.   Role of the Special Envoy for Guantanamo Closure

My responsibilities as Special Envoy for Guantanamo Closure at the Department of State include all diplomatic issues related to the detention facility, including the negotiation of each transfer from the facility. We work closely in this regard, and in following up on transfers from the detention facility, with our Embassies around the world.

The process for transferring Guantanamo detainees is thorough and rigorous. From the very beginning of this Administration we have and continue to implement stringent processes and procedures to determine whether a detainee should be approved for transfer that include multiple layers of review by career national security professionals. I will summarize how decisions are made on whether a detainee should be transferred or remain in detention, as well as the extensive interagency efforts undertaken to achieve a security framework that is suitable for the specific detainee and compliant with statutory requirements before each transfer. Finally, I hope to dispel any misconceptions regarding the Administration's track-record to date in regard to detainee reengagement.

III.   How We Negotiate Transfers

Working with the other departments and agencies involved in Guantanamo transfers, we have continued to negotiate appropriate security and humane treatment assurances for those detainees who are approved for transfer. Since I took office one year ago yesterday, we have transferred 37 detainees to 11 countries. We expect to make substantial progress in transferring many of the remaining approved-for-transfer detainees by the end of the summer, in a manner that protects our national security and is consistent with our long-standing policy on humane treatment.

Decisions regarding whether, when, and where to transfer a detainee are the culmination of a rigorous interagency process. The Department of State leads diplomatic negotiations with foreign governments regarding the transfer of Guantanamo detainees, but we are typically joined in our efforts by senior career officials from the Departments of Defense, Justice, and Homeland Security, as well as those in the Intelligence Community and on the Joint Staff. Generally, transfer negotiations occur in two steps. First, the U.S. government obtains a political commitment that the potential receiving country is willing in principle to resettle or repatriate a detainee or detainees, and to impose various security measures that will substantially mitigate the threat the detainee or detainees may pose after their transfer. In the second step, we engage in technical discussions with the foreign officials responsible for implementing these measures. The higher-level meetings provide us the opportunity to convey our expectations to the potential host nation and to assess our potential partner's political will. The technical discussions offer the opportunity to tailor integration and security measures to specific circumstances under consideration, to share best practices from previous detainee transfers and, perhaps most importantly, to determine, based on an individualized assessment of these specific circumstances, whether the statutory standard in the National Defense Authorization Act governing the foreign transfer of Guantanamo detainees can be met.

Simultaneously, U.S. agencies update the assessment of the potential transferee, drawing upon all reasonably available information on a detainee in possession of the United States. We also provide our foreign partners with updated assessment of the detainees under consideration and offer them the opportunity to travel to Guantanamo to interview potential transferees. Throughout the process, we work to ensure that we achieve a security framework that is suitable for the specific detainee(s) under consideration for transfer and satisfies or exceeds the statutory requirements for transfers, including that the receiving government has taken or will take steps to substantially mitigate the threat these specific individuals may pose after being transferred.

Once we conclude our diplomatic negotiations that will result in a security framework that we assess will substantially mitigate the threat that a detainee may pose after transfer, the Secretary of Defense consults with the Secretaries of State, and Homeland Security, the Attorney General, the Director of National Intelligence, and the Chairman of the Joint Chiefs of Staff on the transfer. Only after the Secretary of Defense receives the views of those Principals—and only if he is satisfied that the requirements of the National Defense Authorization Act are satisfied— does the Secretary of Defense sign and transmit a certification to Congress conveying his intent to transfer detainees.

IV.   Challenges

Many of the detainees approved for transfer cannot be returned to their home country due to security or humane treatment concerns. Consequently, it is necessary to resettle detainees in countries of which they are not nationals. Executing such resettlements requires intense diplomacy and careful attention to security and integration measures. Of the 29 detainees currently approved for transfer, 22 are from Yemen. Members of this Committee are aware of the security situation in that country. The Administration has not transferred a Guantanamo detainee to Yemen since 2010, and our focus is on resettling Yemeni nationals in third countries. These individuals should not remain in Guantanamo solely because of their nationality, if the U.S. government has otherwise concluded that they can and should be transferred subject to appropriate security and humane treatment assurances. Since January 1, 2015, we have resettled 39 Yemenis to six countries on three continents. It is a testament to our strong standing internationally that numerous countries have been willing to provide homes for those individuals who cannot be returned to their own country and who should not remain in detention solely because of the country of their birth.

V.   Reengagement

According to the most recent unclassified intelligence community report pursuant to Section 307 of the 2012 Intelligence Authorization Act, less than 5 percent of those detainees transferred by this Administration—seven (one of whom is dead) out of 144—are *confirmed* of engaging in terrorist or insurgent activity following their release from Guantanamo.[5] 8.3 percent—that is 12, including one who is dead, of 144—are *suspected* of engaging in terrorist or insurgent activity following their release from Guantanamo. Although we would prefer that no former detainees engage in such activity following their release, the low rate of reengagement for detainees released since January 20, 2009, is testament to the rigorous, interagency approach the Administration has taken to both approving detainees for transfer and to negotiating and vetting detainee transfer frameworks.

---

[5] OFFICE OF THE DIRECTOR OF NATIONAL INTELLIGENCE, SUMMARY OF THE REENGAGEMENT OF DETAINEES FORMERLY HELD AT GUANTANAMO BAY, CUBA (March 2016).

VI. Closing the Detention Facility at Guantanamo Bay is a Bipartisan National Security Imperative

Lastly, closing the detention facility at Guantanamo Bay is a national security imperative, and should not be portrayed as partisan issue.

Even before President Obama took office, President Bush concluded that continued operation of Guantanamo damages our national security. He transferred over 500 detainees out of Guantanamo during his two terms in office. President Obama reached the same conclusion for many of the same reasons that led President Bush to begin emptying Guantanamo of detainees.

The continued operation of this facility has significantly impacted our credibility in the international community, and world leaders and organizations—from the Pope to the Organization for American States, consistently call on the United States to close GTMO. Its continued operation undermines our moral leadership and is an irritant to critical bilateral relationships. President Obama recently stated that, "[w]hen I talk to other world leaders, they bring up the fact that Guantanamo is not resolved."[6] He went on to note that, "[a]s President, I have spent countless hours dealing with this . . . . Our closest allies have raised it with me continually. They often raise specific cases of detainees repeatedly."[7] I am sure this information comes as no surprise to this Committee.

The bipartisan view that Guantanamo harms national security is not limited to Presidents Obama and Bush. Their conclusion that Guantanamo should be closed is shared by Senator John McCain, who has remarked that he is "in favor of closing Guantanamo because of the image that Guantanamo has in the world, whether it's deserved or not,"[8] as well as by Secretary Kerry. Likewise former Secretaries of State Clinton, Rice, Powell, Albright, Christopher, Baker, and Henry Kissinger[9] have all advocated for closing Guantanamo. Secretaries of Defense Carter, Panetta, and Gates have similarly all advocated for closing the detention facility, as have three former Chairmen of the Joint Chiefs of Staff, and 42 retired Generals and Admirals.

VII. Conclusion

Thank you again, ladies and gentlemen of the Committee. I greatly appreciate the opportunity to speak to you about this important issue. I look forward to your questions, and to a more detailed discussion in closed session.

---

[6] President Barack Obama, Remarks by the President on Plan to Close the Prison at Guantanamo Bay (Feb. 23, 2016), *available at* https://www.whitehouse.gov/the-press-office/2016/02/23/remarks-president-plan-close-prison-guantanamo-bay.

[7] *Id.*

[8] Jacqueline Klimas, *Republicans Offer Obama Path to Close Guantanamo Before Leaving Office*, WASH. TIMES, May 14, 2015.

[9] *Shut Jail, Ex-Diplomats Say: Powell, Kissinger, Albright, Baker and Christopher*, L.A. TIMES, Mar. 28, 2008, at A15.

Chairman ROYCE. Thank you.

Mr. Lewis.

STATEMENT OF MR. PAUL M. LEWIS, SPECIAL ENVOY FOR GUANTANAMO DETENTION CLOSURE, U.S. DEPARTMENT OF DEFENSE

Mr. LEWIS. Chairman Royce, Ranking Member Engel, distinguished members of the committee, Representative Donovan, thank you for the opportunity to testify again regarding the administration's Guantanamo detainee transfer process.

Secretary Carter has approved the transfer of 43 detainees, 28 of whom have been transferred this year. Secretary Hagel approved the transfer of 44 detainees. Secretary Panetta, 7, and Secretary Gates, 65.

During this administration, 159 detainees have been transferred. Mr. Chairman, we understand the importance of this issue to you and this committee and we appreciate the attention you have given to it.

As I stated in March at the outset, I'd like to reiterate one continuing fundamental point regarding this detention facility. The President and his National Security Committee have determined that closing this detention facility is a national security imperative.

Imperative is a strong term. The President in his leadership of the national security team believe that the continued operation of the detention facility weakens our national security.

Closing Guantanamo is about protecting the country, not weakening it. As you know, the importance in closing this detention facility is echoed by former President George W. Bush and a long list of former Secretaries of State, Secretaries of Defense, Joint Staff Chairmen, and other former military leaders.

As Representative Engel noted, a letter was provided to the committee by former flag officers, including a former commandant of the Marine Corps. Transfers from Gitmo are in the national security interest of the United States and are conducted in a safe and responsible manner.

On March 23, 2016, I testified before this committee. During that hearing, as the chairman noted, I was asked whether the Department of Defense had ever knowingly transferred a detainee to a country that did not exhibit an ability to substantially mitigate the risk or control the individual.

In response to that question, I stated that the Department of Defense had not conducted such a transfer. I stand by my response.

We have addressed your concerns, Mr. Chairman, in the letter that we sent to you this week and I, again, apologize for the late response. But I want to briefly highlight several points.

Here's our statutory framework: The 2016 NDAA requires that at least 30 days prior to any transfer and in addition to other requirements the Secretary of Defense certify to Congress that the receiving country has taken or agreed to take steps to substantially mitigate any risk that the individual could attempt to re-engage or otherwise threaten the United States. We have met that statutory requirement with each of our transfers.

Prior to the transfer of any detainee to a foreign country, the United States Government receives security assurances from the receiving country regarding the actions that the receiving country has taken or agrees to take to substantially mitigate the risk.

After the assurances are negotiated, the Secretary of Defense and his senior staff engage in a robust review process that considers many factors, including all of the intelligence that the government has regarding the threat posed by the individual detainee and the security assurances.

Importantly, updated intelligence, medical, and compliance information is provided to each country regarding the detainees under consideration for the transfer. Many countries also take the opportunity to travel to Gitmo to interview transfer candidates.

After full consideration of all this information, including a full and updated assessment from the intelligence community, the Secretary makes the determination to that I told you about earlier.

As Secretary Carter has testified and Secretary Hagel testified, they take this responsibility very seriously. Secretary Carter has said he will not transfer a detainee that he does not believe is in the security interests of the United States to do so.

These transfers have not been conducted in a vacuum, sir. Each transfer is formally notified to Congress and we regularly brief members and staff on transfers.

With the notice of each transfer we offer to brief congressional leadership and members and staff of all the national security committees. I appreciate the opportunity we have had to regularly brief you and your staff regarding these transfers.

Briefly, I think it is important to put these recent transfer decisions on foreign policy context for this committee. Many countries in the international community want to close Gitmo and have stepped up to help us.

Specifically, over 30 countries since 2009 have accepted for resettlement Guantanamo detainees that are not nationals of their country.

Additionally, there is sustained support for our closure efforts from civil society organizations, both domestic and abroad, including the Organization for American States. Even the Vatican has expressed the support for our closure efforts.

In summary, each transfer is only approved after careful scrutiny by the intensive interagency review process and the negotiation of the security assurances sufficient to substantially mitigate any threat.

Finally, I'd like to take a moment to again recognize the military service members who conduct detention operations at Guantanamo. These men and women continue to have our deepest appreciation for their service and the professionalism they display each and every day on behalf of our Nation.

Thank you, Mr. Chairman. I look forward to your questions.

[The prepared statement of Mr. Lewis follows:]

STATEMENT OF

PAUL M. LEWIS

SPECIAL ENVOY FOR GUANTANAMO DETENTION CLOSURE
U.S. DEPARTMENT OF DEFENSE

BEFORE THE HOUSE COMMITTEE ON FOREIGN AFFAIRS
JULY 7, 2016

Chairman Royce, Ranking Member Engel, distinguished members of the committee, thank you for the opportunity testify again regarding the Administration's Guantanamo detainee transfer process and plan to close the Guantanamo Bay detention facility.

I am pleased to join my colleague Lee Wolosky, the Department of State Special Envoy for Guantanamo Detention Closure.

Overview

There are **79** detainees remaining at the Guantanamo Bay detention facility. Of these, **29** are currently eligible for transfer, **10** are being prosecuted or have been sentenced, and **40** are in the process of being reviewed by the Periodic Review Board processes.

Secretary of Defense Carter has approved the transfer of **43** detainees – **28** of whom have been transferred this year. Secretary Hagel approved the transfer of **44** detainees, Secretary Panetta 7 and Secretary Gates **65**. During this Administration **159** detainees have been transferred.

Closure Is a National Security Imperative

At the outset I want to reiterate one continuing fundamental point regarding the detention facility at Guantanamo Bay. The President and his national security team have determined that closing this detention facility is a national security imperative. The President and the leadership of his national security team believe that the continued operation of the detention facility at Guantanamo weakens our national security by damaging our relationships with key allies and partners, draining resources, and providing violent extremists with a propaganda tool.

As you know, this view is shared by former President George W. Bush, and a long list of former secretaries of state, defense, Joint Staff chairmen, and other former military leaders.

These transfers are in the national security interest of the United States and are conducted in a safe and responsible manner.

Prior Testimony

On March 23, 2016, I testified before this Committee. During that hearing, I was asked whether the Department of Defense had ever knowingly transferred a detainee to a country that did not exhibit an ability to substantially mitigate the risk of recidivism or maintain control of that individual. In response to that question, I stated the Department of Defense had not conducted such a transfer. I stand by my response.

We have addressed the concerns of the Chairman's letter of May 16, 2016 in our recent response, but I would like to take the time to briefly highlight several key points.

The 2016 NDAA requires that, at least 30 days prior to any transfer and in addition to other requirements, the Secretary of Defense certify to Congress that the receiving country has taken or has agreed to take steps to substantially mitigate any risk the individual could attempt to reengage in terrorist activity or otherwise threaten the United States or its allies or interests. The previous requirement, found in §1035 of the 2014 NDAA, likewise required the Secretary of Defense to make a determination that actions that have been taken or are planned to be taken will substantially mitigate the risk of the individual engaging or reengaging in any terrorist or other hostile activity that threatens the United States, or United States persons or interests.

Prior to the transfer of any detainee to a foreign country, the United States Government receives security assurances from the receiving country regarding the actions that the receiving country has taken or agrees to take to substantially mitigate the risk of reengagement. The Department of State has the primary responsibility for negotiating these security assurances with foreign countries. I and others at the Department of Defense work closely with the Department of State in negotiating these assurances.

After the assurances are negotiated, the Secretary of Defense then engages in a robust review process that considers among other things, the assessments of the intelligence community regarding the threat posed by the individual detainee and the security assurances negotiated with the foreign government,

Importantly, updated intelligence, medical, and compliance information is provided to each country regarding detainees under consideration for transfer. Many countries also take the opportunity to travel to GTMO and interview transfer candidates.

If the receiving country has previously taken a detainee who subsequently reengaged in terrorism, the Secretary also specifically considers that in making his determination, including any substantive adjustments to the receiving government's approach to transfers as a result of the experience gained from the previous transfer(s), to include any additional mitigation or corrective measures that can be put in place to address the specific threat that may be posed by former or prospective transferees. As part of this review process and prior to a final determination, the Secretary consults with

the Director of National Intelligence, the Attorney General, the Secretary of Homeland
Security, the Secretary of State, and the Chairman of the Joint Chiefs of Staff on the
proposed transfer.

After full consideration of all of this information, including a full and up-to-date
assessment from the intelligence community, the Secretary makes a determination
whether the transfer is in the national security interest of the United States and that the
receiving country has taken or agreed to take appropriate steps to substantially mitigate
any risk the individual could attempt to reengage in terrorist activity or otherwise threaten
the United States or its allies or interests. Reference has been made by the committee to
specific intelligence reports. Again, I want to emphasize that the Secretary of Defense
considers an up-to-date assessment based on the totality of information available, and
consults with the Secretaries of State, and Homeland Security, the Attorney General, the
Director of National Intelligence, and the Chairman of the Joint Chiefs of Staff.

For each approved transfer that I have been involved with, under both Secretary
Carter and Secretary Hagel, the Secretary personally determined and certified that the
relevant statutory requirements were met, including that the foreign government has
taken or agreed to take steps to substantially mitigate the risk of the individual engaging
or reengaging in any terrorist or other hostile activity that threatened the United States.

Both Secretary Carter and Secretary Hagel have testified forcefully on this issue.
Both emphasized their in-depth and rigorous approach to evaluating transfers and the
seriousness with which they approached this responsibility.

Not all detainees can be transferred at this time. That is why I fully support the
President's policy to support legislation authorizing detention for those detainees who

currently cannot be repatriated or resettled, in a secure facility in the United States. We continue to seek meaningful engagement from Congress on the Closure Plan we submitted in February.

These transfers have not been conducted in a vacuum. Each transfer is formally notified to Congress and we regularly brief Members and staff on transfers. With the notice of each transfer, we offer to brief congressional leadership and members and staff of all the national security committees. I appreciate the opportunity we have had to regularly brief you and your staff regarding these transfers.

Recent Transfer Decisions in a Foreign Policy Context

Briefly, I think it is important to put recent transfer decisions in a foreign policy context for this committee. Many countries in the international community want us to close the Guantanamo Bay detention facility and many have stepped up to help in this process. Overall, thirty countries since 2009 have accepted for resettlement Guantanamo detainees who are not nationals of their country.

There is broad support in the international community for closure of the detention facility, in addition to the thirty resettlement countries, an additional thirteen have received their own nationals from Guantanamo.

Additionally, there is sustained support for our closure efforts from civil society organizations, both domestically and abroad, and numerous international organizations continue to call on the United States to close Guantanamo, including the Organization of American States. Even the Vatican has expressed its support of our closure efforts.

Conclusion

In summary, each transfer is only approved after careful scrutiny by the intensive interagency review process and the negotiation of security assurances sufficient to substantially mitigate any threat that may be posed by the detainee to the United States and its allies and partners.

Finally, I would like to take a moment to again recognize the military service members conducting detention operations at Guantanamo Bay. These remarkable men and women continue to have our deepest appreciation for their service and the professionalism they display each and every day on behalf of our Nation.

Thank you, and I look forward to your questions.

Chairman ROYCE. Thank you, Mr. Lewis.

The last time you appeared before this committee we asked specific questions about the transfer of detainees to countries ill equipped to handle them.

Specifically, we asked whether the Department of Defense ever transferred a detainee to a country that it knew was incapable of maintaining control of that individual and keeping him from returning to the battlefield. Mr. Lewis responded no, Mr. Wolosky stated that he was not aware of such an instance.

Upon further review of your own intelligence assessments, those answers appear to be false. In fact, it appears that the administration has released dangerous terrorists to ill-equipped countries on numerous occasions.

On May 16, I wrote to your departments asking you to correct the record. You did not. The committee asked the administration to halt all transfers until you explained your testimony. You did not.

In fact, you completely ignored the letter until we called this hearing and that is why we are here today. And I am going to ask you several simple questions and I'd appreciate a simple yes or no answer.

Mr. Lewis, Mr. Wolosky, in your roles do you have access to intelligence assessments of detainees and transfer countries?

Mr. LEWIS. Yes.

Chairman ROYCE. Do you review those intelligence assessments prior to the transfer of detainees to the custody of foreign governments?

Mr. LEWIS. Yes, sir.

Mr. WOLOSKY. We review the intelligence assessments that are material to the issue before us, which is whether to transfer a detainee to a specific country under certain circumstances in order to be able to meet the statutory standard.

Chairman ROYCE. Right. And in my May 16th letter I referenced three intelligence reports submitted to Congress pursuant to Section 1023 of the National Defense Authorization Act, those reports are dated May 31, 2013, July 15, 2014, August 6, 2015. Are you familiar with the content of those reports?

Mr. WOLOSKY. Yes.

Mr. LEWIS. Yes.

Chairman ROYCE. Are you aware that those reports contains assessments of each country to which the Defense Department has transferred detainees?

Mr. WOLOSKY. Yes.

Mr. LEWIS. Yes.

Chairman ROYCE. And are you aware that those assessments indicate that some countries lack the ability to control those terrorists?

Mr. WOLOSKY. We cannot by law discuss classified Defense Intelligence Agency assessments in this session, Mr. Chairman. We're happy to do that in closed session.

What I would point out to the committee is that in connection with each transfer we do rely on intelligence reporting that is broader than just DIA reporting and as I said it is tailored specifically to the issue of a transfer to a certain country at a particular point in time and is geared toward a determination or an analysis of whether the relevant statutory standard for transfers can be met.

Mr. LEWIS. Mr. Chairman, the reports you refer to are one of many reports we look at. We look at all source information from the intelligence community and as the Envoy has stated, the Secretary makes his determination looking at all the evidence that is available, the updated evidence, and in particular he makes his assessment after we overlay the security assurances to that country.

So if the intelligence tells us that there may be a gap in capabilities that is what we negotiate the assurances for. So again, we look at those records, Mr. Chairman. But we look at a much broader array of records.

Chairman ROYCE. I am going to explain to you, Mr. Lewis, that is not what you said here in March, all right. And in light of your familiarity with the intelligence reports and what is in those reports, I am just going to ask you again: Has the administration ever transferred a detainee to a country it knew was incapable of monitoring that individual or preventing him from traveling outside the country or otherwise keeping him from returning to the battlefield?

Mr. LEWIS. Sir, since I've worked for Secretary Hagel and Secretary Carter, every transfer has met the statutory requirement and it is my understanding that the administration, prior to my coming, transfer pursuant to the process that Envoy Wolosky indicated and there are no transfers that I am aware of that did not meet the statutory requirement.

Chairman ROYCE. I don't think you can just wish away intelligence reports that raise grave concerns, reports that you chose to deny when asked about them in our last hearing.

But if you're now saying that the intelligence reports are—I assume the implication here—incomplete, then I have to say from what we can tell the President has made a political decision to close Guantanamo no matter what the cost to national security based upon our experience, based upon our discussions which go on for some considerable time now in terms of the warnings from us on this committee about the five individuals who were transferred to Uruguay and their subsequent conduct and now the fact that one of them has been released.

That can be the only reason why these intelligence assessments are being pushed aside, in my judgement. And it appears that the assurances that you got from Uruguay didn't account for anything.

This fellow, Jihad Diyab, walked right out of Uruguay. We have no idea where he is, and if that country is telling you that they won't prevent their travel, which is what I pointed out to you, then we'd better listen.

If they are not going to prevent their travel then it is not a surprise what subsequently has occurred. So Mr. Wolosky, you have briefed this committee several times about Uruguay. You have told us repeatedly that the Government of Uruguay was capable of handling these terrorists.

In fact, you testified on March 23rd that "we are confident, to your question, that the Government of Uruguay is taking appropriate steps to substantially mitigate the risk associated with each of the six detainees that have been transferred to its custody.'' That turned out to be wrong, as I've pointed out.

Jihad Diyab has now escaped. Now, the other point I would make out may make to you, and this also goes to some of the conversations he's had, is that I am aware this was the third time he left Uruguay and nobody knows where he is.

The media is reporting that he could be on his way to Syria or Yemen. And I would just like to ask: Why did you provide false assurances to Congress? Why did you mislead us about Uruguay's capabilities? Because I made it very clear to you our concerns about Uruguay's capabilities. They were pretty up front.

Mr. WOLOSKY. Mr. Chairman, I strongly disagree with any suggestion that I misled this committee. In fact, I stand by my testimony from March in which I affirmed that Uruguay had committed to and is in fact taking steps to substantially mitigate the risk of the six detainees that were transferred to its custody in December 2014.

While we would have preferred that Mr. Diyab remained in Uruguay, if in fact he is not in Uruguay currently, until the expiration of the 2-year resettlement program that was the subject of the agreement reached with Uruguay and reached with him, frankly, the fact is is that the standard is not elimination of risk.

It is mitigation of risk, and we never represented to this committee that there was a travel prohibition.

What the President's closure plan describes generally, and I cannot get into this forum—into the specific assurances provided by the Government of Uruguay, but what the President's plan describes are travel restrictions.

The President's plan describes specifically the withholding of international travel documents.

Now, there are a number of additional steps that we take and our partners take to restrict travel and to monitor travel. I cannot go into those in an open session.

I am happy to describe them to you even in this specific context of Uruguay in a closed session. But I cannot do it here.

Chairman ROYCE. But let me explain this simple fact to you. When a country tells you that they won't prevent a terrorist from traveling then you had better listen if your intention is to release that terrorist into that country.

But my time has expired. I will go to Mr. Eliot Engel of New York.

Mr. ENGEL. Thank you, Mr. Chairman.

Mr. Lewis, let me start with you. In a hearing before this committee in March you discussed the issue of former Guantanamo detainees killing Americans.

According to White House Press Secretary Josh Earnest, none of the former detainees who have gone through a screening process implemented by this administration in the 2009 have harmed Americans.

To quote Mr. Earnest, from March of this year, and I quote him, ''No one who's been released from prison at Guantanamo Bay on President Obama's watch has been implicated in violence against Americans.''

So I would like to ask both of you: How has the Obama administration changed the detainee transfer process from the process used before President Obama took office, or has he not changed it?

I understand it is been changed. How have these changes helped prevent former detainees from harming Americans? So why don't we start with you, Mr. Wolosky?

Mr. WOLOSKY. Sure. Thank you, Congressman Engel. Five hundred and thirty-two detainees from Guantanamo were released under the administration of George W. Bush. The fact is that we can't tell you much about the circumstances under which they were released.

We can speak to what our administration has done and what we understand to have been the process in the previous administration.

So first, we engage in a rigorous interagency evidence-based process reliant predominantly on career government officials to determine first if a detainee may in principle be designated as approved for transfer.

That's the first step. This is an interagency process that includes many career professionals throughout the government and as I describe in my testimony in this administration there are actually two separate processes at various points in the administration to first determine whether in principle a detainee may be safely transferred, subject to security assurances.

Second thing we do, very carefully, is we negotiate for detainees who have been approved for transfer specific security assurance packages consistent with local law in the places that we transfer these detainees to and after obtaining a political commitment from the country in question that under the circumstances in question the measures to be put in place by the country—monitoring, travel restrictions, information sharing, integration planning—will mitigate substantially the risk that that particular detainee may pose.

That's what we do, and what we have done, as I said in my opening statement, has reduced the re-engagement rate, the confirmed rate to under 5 percent. It's much higher in the previous administration.

We believe that that reflects the fact that the things that I just described simply weren't done in the previous administration. But that is what we have done. Thank you.

Mr. LEWIS. Mr. Engel, it is a more rigorous process. The process in the previous administration was only DoD—primarily only DoD, as Envoy Wolosky has said, this is interagency.

When the Obama administration took office there were about 240 detainees at Gitmo. We took a fresh look for over a year at all those detainees and decided three categories—those that could be eligible for transfer with appropriate security assurances to the proper country, those that they wanted to refer for prosecution to take a look at prosecution, and those that merited continued law of war detention.

I say it is more rigorous because as Lee said, there's a broader group of career professionals and some political but primarily career professionals, intelligence folks, career prosecutors, who looked at these cases.

They also looked at a broader array of evidence. They looked at all the evidence that the USG possessed whereas the previous process was primarily DoD evidence.

And then as we know, Congress weighed in. We now have the statutory overlay for all transfers. So the bottom line is, as Lee said, it is a much more rigorous and intensive process.

Mr. ENGEL. Thank you. You know, I think it is important to put it into context because, look, even one prisoner escaping is one prisoner too much. So we are not going to say that anything is foolproof.

Nothing is foolproof. But I think that if we look and see what the administration has done and the safeguards that they have tried to put in, I feel that we are absolutely doing our best and in fact it is a big improvement than the previous administration.

So let me ask you this. We've heard a lot about the challenges of closing Guantanamo. It is true that some former detainees have re-engaged. I know the chairman is very upset about it and so am I.

But can you help put those cases into context? What are the costs of keeping this facility open and how would halting the transfer of cleared detainees affect terrorist recruitment and propaganda and coalition efforts to degrade and defeat terrorist organizations?

Mr. LEWIS. Sir, there are three costs. It's primarily—it drains our expenses, it is wildly, wildly expensive. We can do it cheaper in the United States.

More importantly, for this committee, our allies want us to close Gitmo. It hurts us with the international community. In my previous testimony and in my opening statement I outlined indications in which members of the previous administration at the Department of State said Gitmo hurt us and I believe it is a propaganda and recruiting tool. President Bush said that. Many others have said that.

The bottom fundamental point is we want to protect the country and the national security leadership of this administration, President Bush and many people in his administration, numerous Secretaries of Defense, numerous Secretaries of State, the prior military officials that we talked about including a commandant in the Marine Corps, have said the cost of Gitmo outweighs the benefit.

It hurts us. It hurts us with the international community. It hurts us with our taxpayer money and it is a recruiting tool. The President has made this decision and the national security community leadership has made this decision. Lee?

Mr. WOLOSKY. Sure. Thank you. First, I agree with the Special Envoy's comments and I do feel compelled just to address this notion of terrorists escaping and prisoners escaping and things of that sort.

Just to remind the committee that the individuals that we are talking about were held in law-of-war detention by the United States. They were lawfully held under law-of-war detention.

But they weren't convicted of crimes. When we transfer them to foreign countries we transfer them subject to security assurances such as travel restrictions. This is what this administration does. The previous administration did not do this.

There are a large number of detainees of the 532 transferred in the previous administration, certainly, that weren't even subject to the travel restrictions that we put in place on these individuals.

But, again, just want to make sure that we are getting the terminology right because escaping connotes incarceration. When we transfer individuals who the U.S. Government writ large has concluded may be transferred subject to security assurances they are transferred subject to those security assurances and at that point they are not prisoners. They are former detainees under supervision.

Mr. ENGEL. I will stop now because I know my time has run out. But I wanted to—you know, the thing that irks the chairman and, in fact, frankly, irks all of us is the fact that this person was sent to Uruguay, and Uruguay, apparently doesn't have the ability to monitor this person who now has left the country. Just briefly, could you talk a little bit about the case or do you need to do it in a classified setting?

Mr. WOLOSKY. On the issue of foreign countries' surveillance capabilities, I would need to discuss that with you in closed session and I welcome the opportunity to do so so that you may be informed about what those capabilities are and what they aren't and how they were used and applied in this instance.

Mr. LEWIS. I echo the Envoy's comments. We would appreciate the opportunity to discuss this in detail. What I can tell you is we talked to the Uruguayan authorities on a regular basis. We regularly review intelligence. We regularly look at this and Secretary Hagel, who you know is a very forceful, careful, deliberate person, signed the congressional notification saying he felt that Uruguay could substantially mitigate any threat by this detainee. Again, we are happy to discuss this in closed session.

Mr. ENGEL. I would like to do that in closed session. So I am sure we'll make arrangements to do that. Thank you, Mr. Chairman.

Chairman ROYCE. We'll make arrangements to do that. At the same time, at the end of the day, the Uruguayans gave them the travel cards. Gave them the travel card to travel. At the end of the day, he walked right out of there three times and this time nobody can locate him to get him back into custody and he's an al-Qaeda-linked terrorist. Anyway, I'll go to Ileana Ros-Lehtinen of Florida.

Ms. ROS-LEHTINEN. Thank you so much, Chairman Royce, for calling this hearing and for continuing to demand transparency and accountability from the administration regarding its plans for naval station Guantanamo Bay and the detention center.

As you point out, Mr. Chairman, the administration has not been forthcoming with the American people about the release of dangerous terrorists to various nations. The reality is that the situation is far different than what we've been told.

So I continue to ask myself why does a nation like Uruguay, why does a nation like Ghana, why does a nation like Senegal, as so many others, why would they want to take in these dangerous terrorists unless they believe that the benefits outweigh the risk? Unless the administration convinced them that the benefits outweighed the risk.

And not only that, we are talking about a high-risk, high-threat individual and that person has experience in evading authorities, will conduct operations, going to nations that have limited intelligence that do not possess the most sophisticated monitoring system.

That was obvious with the Uruguay transfer. And we are to believe that the terrorists will not use that to their advantage? That they will be properly overseen? It would probably take them just 1 day to realize how lax the security is in Uruguay, for example.

So it is not a surprise, I think, to any of us that one of these individuals managed to flee Uruguay, where we now know that his movement was not required to be restricted, to Brazil and from there from who knows.

As the chairman said, he may be en route to Syria or there already. So I would ask you if it is possible to get a yes or no answer, has the administration promised any of these countries, whether it is Uruguay, Ghana, Senegal, whatever, cash for taking in these individuals and if so how much, how often, and to which countries?

Mr. WOLOSKY. Congresswoman, we have provided de minimis resettlement assistance to certain countries to support expenditures such as language training, vocational training, things of that sort.

That is fully disclosed to the Congress in the congressional notifications that you receive.

Ms. ROS-LEHTINEN. And if you could refresh my memory for Uruguay, for example, how much would that country have gotten for language and to the other——

Mr. WOLOSKY. I can't tell you off the top of my head but we are happy to provide that information to you supplementally.

Ms. ROS-LEHTINEN. I will get the notification—refresh my memory. Has the administration offered any other favorable agreements or offered to support these countries on other related matters in exchange and if so what kind of exchanges?

Mr. WOLOSKY. Nothing financial beyond what is in the congressional notifications. Anything related is a broad category.

I can say generally in open session that many of our partners do view a detainee transfer as an opportunity to deepen security and counterterrorism and intelligence cooperation with the United States. We generally welcome that and we look to facilitate that interest where it exists.

Ms. ROS-LEHTINEN. And has the administration provided military equipment or military training in exchange for taking in a detainee and if so to what extent and to which governments?

Mr. WOLOSKY. No, not to my knowledge. Paul?

Mr. LEWIS. Ma'am, that is something we'd have to talk about in a closed session.

Ms. ROS-LEHTINEN. Like night vision goggles or something like that?

Mr. LEWIS. Again, the negotiation of the security assurances is very detailed and complex and to discuss any specifics I'd have to talk to you about that in a closed session and we are happy to do so.

Ms. ROS-LEHTINEN. Has the administration provided intelligence equipment or training or promised or offered intelligence sharing to any government in exchange for accepting a detainee and if so to what extent and which governments?

Mr. WOLOSKY. We would have to talk about intelligence matters in closed session.

Ms. ROS-LEHTINEN. So it seems to me that the absence of any of these agreements wouldn't need to be discussed in a classified setting. So, I mean, unless you say no to these questions I think it would be fair to assume that at least some of this has been happening, is happening.

Is it the intent of the Obama administration to continue to release all but a handful of the most dangerous detainees in order to then say to Congress, well, why keep Gitmo open when we have such few detainees there? As if President Obama had not had anything to do with clearing out the number of detainees in the first place.

Mr. WOLOSKY. We intend to continue essentially the policy of the previous administration to transfer detainees that we conclude may be safely and responsibly transferred outside the custody of the United States in accordance with applicable law.

Ms. ROS-LEHTINEN. Would it be fair to say that from now until the end of this Presidency that we would be seeing more and more detainees being released—five, 12, two—until there's just a handful and say hey, look at all this wasted money for just a handful of folks, when you're the ones pushing them out?

Mr. WOLOSKY. We have 29 detainees who are approved for transfer and our intention is to work to transfer those individuals subject to security assurances.

Ms. ROS-LEHTINEN. Thank you. Well, as you know, there's a great deal of resistance about having them come to the United States. Thank you so much, Mr. Chairman.

Chairman ROYCE. Thank you, Ileana Ros-Lehtinen.

We go to Mr. Brad Sherman of California.

Mr. SHERMAN. Okay. I would like to comment on this over the next 5 minutes and I'll probably offend both political parties. The prior administration did release more terrorists than the current administration.

More of those released by the prior administration have been caught fighting us on the battlefield. The fact is, much as we like to fight as Democrats and Republicans, the policy has been the same in both administrations.

House them only in Guantanamo because we don't have the political guts to house them here in the United States and release as many as possible—far too many, far too quickly, and massively understate the costs of the release.

We are told that it is wrong to keep them there for the duration of the war because the war has lasted too long. That is their fault. They waged war against America and no, we never guaranteed them that the war would be short. The purpose of incarcerating POWs is not only to keep them off the battlefield but to deter their comrades.

When we tell the terrorists around the world if you get caught you'll get released while the war is still going on, we encourage their recruitment.

Now, we are told that there are only 12 identified circumstances when Americans have died because of this release. That is such a massive undercount. First of all, when we release somebody and they rejoin the battlefield, do they send us a report?

Are they listed on LinkedIn? New status, rejoined the terrorist movement? And then when one of them at least—when an American dies on the battlefield do we get a report from the terrorists, here's a list of the people who killed him—here's a list of the people who provided them with logistics—here are the people that provided the recruiting—here are the people that provided the financing?

So I would—unless we are certain that one of these released people is being monitored and is not doing anything to help the terrorists we have to assume that they are waging war against us as they did before and the cost of release is also the incredible concessions—Ileana Ros-Lehtinen brought this to our attention.

All the winks, all the nods. Every country in the world, especially small countries, no. Take one detainee. The President of the United States is personally indebted to you and when you've got a fishing concern or if you're seeking something from the United States now or later, the answer is yes. We'll never get an accounting of that because you can't account for the winks and the nods.

Now, we are told that Gitmo is a—that we get a tremendous propaganda advantage if Gitmo is closed. Of course, we only partially closed it.

We have no propaganda advantage. It's still a symbol the other side can use as long as it is open with one detainee. But we could bring these prisoners to the United States. That does not enhance their legal status.

The Supreme Court has ruled in the Boumediene case and the Hamdan case that they have just as many legal rights there as they would here.

But we—here's an America where we accepted nuclear bases in our States knowing that they were targets for the Soviet Union and now we can't even accept a prisoner and we whip up all this fury.

We have 443 convicted terrorists in American prisons right now. I'll ask our witnesses to raise their hands if they are aware of any of those that escaped. I see no hands going up. I am not aware and I've researched this.

We've got Moussaoui, we've got Tsarnaev, we got the shoe bomber, the underwear bomber, the World Trade Center in 1993 bombers, the Oklahoma City bomber, and the Unabomber, and we are trying to bring to the United States El Chapo, who escaped Mexican prisons twice.

We can incarcerate people here and obtain the political advantage that we are told can be achieved by shutting down Gitmo. But instead we constantly vote on ways to not do it. If the legal rights of these POWs in the United States is too great if they are on U.S. soil, that is the fault of Congress. We can pass laws identifying that these are POWs.

They're nonuniformed enemy combatants and entitled to less protection than those who would wear uniforms fighting against us. So we've got a lot of dead Americans as a result of this catch and release program.

We've got one party who says we can't house them here, although we are able to house terrorists here in our prisons, and

31

we've got another political party so anxious to shut things down that we massively understate the cost of releasing, and I yield back.

Ms. ROS-LEHTINEN. Thank you very much, Mr. Sherman.

Mr. Issa of California.

Mr. ISSA. Thank you, Madam Chair.

I would just like to bring us up to speed in one area. Is it true that under current law, closing Guantanamo is prohibited? This isn't a trick question.

Mr. WOLOSKY. I don't think that current law prohibits closing Guantanamo. I think that what current law prohibits is the expenditure of money to move detainees at Guantanamo into the United States.

Mr. ISSA. Okay. So under current law you can close Guantanamo by releasing the prisoners. You just can't bring them here. That's your assessment?

Mr. WOLOSKY. I believe the current law prohibits detainees from being brought into the United States.

Mr. ISSA. Okay. So the reason that you both have titles that say Special Envoy for Guantanamo Closure is because your job is to close Guantanamo. Is that right?

Mr. WOLOSKY. Sir, that is correct.

Mr. ISSA. Okay. So now I just—I got a yes and that is far enough.

Mr. LEWIS. Sir, my title is Guantanamo Detention Closure. We're not closing the naval facility.

Mr. ISSA. No, I understand that the President who loves Chavez—or loves the Castros enough to open up relations—has not decided to give back what we have in perpetuity. So we'll leave that aside.

Your job is to close the detention. You are working toward that. I just want to ask one or two fairly simple questions.

It's been said many times on both sides of the dais that President George W. Bush's administration released more prisoners actually than you inherited, right? He released more than you have?

Mr. LEWIS. Yes.

Mr. ISSA. Okay. And during that time it has been discovered and during this administration it has been discovered and made public that in fact some released by the Bush administration went back and killed Americans on the battlefield in Afghanistan and other places. Is that correct?

Mr. LEWIS. Yes, sir.

Mr. ISSA. So George W. Bush released more prisoners, attempted to vet them, was wrong. They went back, they killed Americans on the battlefield and we know it and the public knows it, right?

Mr. LEWIS. Yes, sir.

Mr. ISSA. Okay. So George W. Bush's failures are now very public. They released people who went back and killed Americans on the battlefield. Okay. Like Mr. Sherman, that is not necessarily with my party.

This President has released many additional people who have returned to Afghanistan. Are you prepared to say that none of them killed Americans?

Mr. WOLOSKY. You're talking about Guantanamo detainees——

Mr. ISSA. Guantanamo.

Mr. WOLOSKY [continuing]. Returned to Afghanistan in 2009?

Mr. ISSA. Guantanamo detainees released after 2009 who in fact went back and killed Americans.

Mr. WOLOSKY. The assessment of the intelligence community is that no detainees released since 2009 during this administration are responsible for the deaths of Americans.

Mr. ISSA. So your public statement is that no detainees released by this administration have killed Americans on the battlefield as of today?

Mr. WOLOSKY. Correct.

Mr. ISSA. Okay. I just want to make sure I have it on the record because I don't believe it. But you can say it and you're under oath and I believe it that you believe it.

So I just want to make sure we understand. We're sitting here and somehow President George W. Bush early on, releasing the less dangerous, the easier to vet, the less likely to be a hardened criminal terrorist—terrorists, not criminals—they were released. They killed Americans. You're releasing people, they are not killing Americans. How do you account for that? Is this rehabilitation that you've done?

Mr. WOLOSKY. Sir, there are a lot of factual predicates embodied in your question that would require some correction.

Mr. ISSA. Well, President Bush released people. They killed Americans. You released people. They didn't kill Americans on the battlefield. How do you account for that difference that you've said under oath?

Mr. WOLOSKY. As I indicated in my testimony submitted for the record, we have put in place procedures that are comprehensive, they are rigorous, they are interagency in nature and we believe that, as a result, those procedures have contributed to the very substantial reduction in the re-engagement rates seen between both administrations.

Mr. ISSA. Okay. Well, let's do that. You've used procedures that have limited re-engagement. But it hasn't eliminated re-engagement, correct?

Mr. WOLOSKY. That's correct.

Mr. ISSA. So you've released people after 2009. They have re-engaged. They're back on the battlefield attempting to kill Americans, right?

Mr. WOLOSKY. It is not correct to say that anyone who has re-engaged under the definitions used by the intelligence community for confirmed or suspected re-engagement is back on the battlefield.

Again, I am happy to talk or, better yet, the intelligence community can speak to the committee about the standards that are used. But it is an overstatement to say that an individual, for instance, who has been suspected of re-engagement is on the battlefield seeking to do harm to coalition forces.

Mr. ISSA. Okay. But I just—you know, it is just one of these things that I think in a very public—it is not—this is not something that needs to be privately discussed. It's something—now, Madam Chair, if I can have 30 more seconds. My predecessors did.

People that were released under Bush re-engaged and killed Americans. You'll have us believe in a public environment that although people released under this administration were more hardened criminals—these were the people that were in fact not released under Bush because he thought they were too dangerous. They've been released. You're saying in a public forum that they re-engaged but you're saying nobody died.

Mr. WOLOSKY. Sir, again, it is incorrect to assume that individuals released under Bush are less dangerous or more dangerous than released during this administration.

Again, this would require a rather long discussion about why, for instance, the overwhelming preponderance of the detainees who were approved for transfer or who remain in Guantanamo today are from Yemen.

So it is just simply not correct to make blanket assessments about who is more or who is less dangerous or, frankly, what the procedures—you keep talking about vetting done by the Bush administration.

Again, we are not aware of the type of vetting that was done in that administration. So, again, there are a lot of premises embedded in your question.

Mr. ISSA. Thank you, Madam Chair.

Ms. ROS-LEHTINEN. Thank you. Thank you, Mr. Issa.

Mr. Duncan of South Carolina I am sure will follow through.

Mr. DUNCAN. Do you need some more time, the gentleman from California?

Mr. ISSA. Thirty more seconds.

Mr. DUNCAN. You're yielded 30 seconds.

Mr. ISSA. Thank you. I just want to understand. We have heard endlessly that the Bush administration released people and they went back on the battlefield and President George W. Bush and his administration have to live with the fact that they thought these people could be safely released back to Qatar and to other countries and in some cases they were wrong.

But you continued to work toward closure by release back to these countries, Yemen being a particular area of concern, and I just want to make sure the American public hears in an open session that you believe that you have been flawless in that no Americans have died because of people released on this President's watch and you've said that.

So I want to thank the gentleman that was very kind to let me recap.

Mr. DUNCAN. Thank you, and thanks for your approach to everything, Chairman Issa.

I first off want to apologize to the lady with the Department of State for coming across abrasive about another issue and I thank you for your help on that other matter.

We have established the fact that one of the Uruguayan Six has disappeared. We've also established the fact, I think, that there are certain requirements and parameters that must be met before detainees are transferred to a third country.

Uruguay told us—well, first off, Uruguayan law prevented intelligence monitoring and mitigation and former President Mutica said publicly that his government would place no restrictions on the movements of the six detainees that were released to Uruguay.

Later, we had their chief intelligence officer proudly inform the U.S. Embassy that these Uruguayan Six—the Gitmo Six—would not be restricted in any way and that he was not authorized to conduct monitoring or surveillance.

But if we go back to the requirements that have been talked about numerous times here this morning, surveillance and monitoring and some assurances were part of the deal.

So America needs to understand that one of the six detainees captured on the battlefield, al-Qaeda operatives captured either in Tora Bora or Afghanistan, has disappeared. Uruguay, Brazil, United States at this point have no idea where this individual is.

Now, this individual that we are talking about, Jihad Diyab, is a forger. He was responsible for forging documents, passports, travel documents for al-Qaeda terrorists. He's now disappeared into Brazil.

So let's take it to the 30,000-foot level and think about Brazil in general. We've got an area in Brazil and Paraguay known as the tri-border region. A lot of folks are transiting through Latin America through an area known as the tri-border region.

They're coming to South America, to that area, often times on fake passports—not necessarily forged passports, they are just passports that don't belong to them. And they are exchanging those documents in that region for other false documents and trying to transit through Latin America to get to America, to get to the United States.

Case in point—five Syrians traveled to the tri-border region in Brazil on fake Israeli passports. The hypocrisy of that, I think is alarming, that Syrians traveled to the tri-border region on fake Israeli passports, exchanged those documents for somewhere around $25,000 for fake Greek passports that they used to travel to Honduras.

Apprehended in an airport in Honduras trying to come to the United States on fake Greek passports. So now we have a Gitmo detainee forger for al-Qaeda has escaped, disappeared, whatever you want to call it, into Brazil possibly to the tri-border region to assist others from the battlefield.

ISIS operatives, possibly, coming to that area, exchanging documents, getting new forged documents or fake documents to possibly travel to the United States of America. But let's take it another step. There's a huge event getting ready to happen in Brazil known as the Olympics and that is a heck of a terrorist target, folks.

So we've got an al-Qaeda operative who is a forger, who has escaped in Brazil or disappeared in Brazil who has the ability to forge documents and he's in a country that is getting ready to host the Olympics.

I hope our counterterrorism efforts in Brazil, working with our allies there, are full bore.

So I am going to ask, now that this gentleman has escaped—he's gone missing, rather—is the Obama administration concerned about that?

Mr. WOLOSKY. Sir, as I indicated previously, it would have been our preference that all six of the detainees transferred to Uruguay, stayed in Uruguay.

Mr. DUNCAN. You've stated that. I asked you a question. Is the Obama administration concerned over Jihad Diyab's disappearance? Yes or no.

Mr. WOLOSKY. As I said, I would have preferred that he stayed in Uruguay with the five other detainees through the end of the program, which was for another few months until December 2014.

If you're asking me what concerns me, frankly, it is the 532 who were transferred during the previous administration. Without the——

Mr. DUNCAN. We have established the fact that we all wished he would have stayed in Uruguay and would be right there with the other five. What I am asking you is the Obama administration concerned that he has disappeared?

Mr. WOLOSKY. And I believe I've answered your question.

Mr. DUNCAN. Mr. Lewis.

Mr. LEWIS. Sir, we are closely——

Mr. DUNCAN. Okay. Knowing what you know now, will you publicly repudiate the Sloan letter about the Uruguayan concerns so the Uruguayan Government, who this administration tricked, I think, about these people, can finally begin monitoring and controlling the remaining five detainees? Will you repudiate the Sloan letter?

Mr. WOLOSKY. We stand by the Sloan letter and we stand by the representations that we made to the Government of Uruguay at the time of the transfer.

In fact, I believe that the Uruguayans told you, Congressman, when you visited, that they believed the United States had provided accurate information about each of the detainees transferred to their custody.

Mr. DUNCAN. They did, and that contradicted some previous statements they had made publicly. So——

Mr. WOLOSKY. Why do you think that is?

Mr. DUNCAN. I am sorry?

Mr. WOLOSKY. Why do you think that is?

Mr. DUNCAN. We can go back through all of this.

Mr. WOLOSKY. Why would they say one thing to you and another thing privately?

Chairman ROYCE. Mr. Duncan, could you yield for a minute?

Mr. DUNCAN. I can.

Chairman ROYCE. I did want to put something in perspective for our witnesses here and it has to do with why the chairman of the Western Subcommittee would be upset here. And the fact is that the chief of intelligence in Uruguay explained to our committee, gave us the information that they were not allowed to monitor or surveille these six terrorists and the decision you made was to transfer them anyway.

He made that observation to this committee prior to the transfer. You made the decision to transfer these six despite our warnings.

The second point that is upsetting to him is that the intelligence chief was then dismissed from his position after warning us of that and subsequently warning us that they were casing—that they were outside our Embassy after their release and, again, that they were not allowed to monitor or surveille.

Now we find ourselves in the situation—despite Jeff Duncan's admonitions and concerns and despite what we brought up at the prior hearing—we find ourselves in the situation where one of these six terrorists has indeed been able to walk out of Uruguay and no one knows where he is but we do know his attitude and this is the reason for our concern.

But I thank Mr. Duncan for his trips and his work on behalf of the committee.

Mr. DUNCAN. I want to thank the chairman for helping clarify that. The pattern is clear. We have been asking about these Gitmo Six and about the Uruguayans' ability to monitor them for a long time now and we have raised concern about events such as what we've witnessed in the last 60 days where one of the six has just disappeared who was an al-Qaeda terrorist.

There's no doubt about it. He was a forger. And we are supposed to tell these countries that these weren't terrorists, they weren't engaged in attacking or hurting our allies or our United States military in any way. Very clear that he was.

Thank you, Mr. Chairman. I yield back.

Chairman ROYCE. We go to Mr. Matt Salmon of Arizona.

Mr. SALMON. Thank you, Mr. Chairman.

Last time you were here, Mr. Lewis, you testified that Americans have been killed and I am going to piggyback on Mr. Issa and Mr. Duncan's questions.

You subsequently notified the committee that those deaths occurred in Afghanistan by as many as 14 former detainees all who were released by the Bush administration and I'd just like to ask a few questions about that.

How many Americans were killed? Were they U.S. servicemen and -women, civilians or both? What are their names and where are they from?

Mr. LEWIS. Sir, it is our understanding that there are 14 and I can get you the specifics on that. I believe we've—the intelligence community can get you those specific details. But the number is 14. Many of the incidents were in large-scale firefights in a war zone.

So we can't always distinguish whether Americans were killed by former detainees or other participants. But the intelligence community can get you the specific details that you asked for, sir.

Mr. SALMON. Okay. And just to recap the specifics, I'd like to know whether they were servicemen or servicewomen or civilians or both and I'd like to know what their names are and where they are from. Those are the things I'd like and you can provide or get me all of that?

Mr. LEWIS. Yes, sir.

Mr. SALMON. That'll be very, very helpful. And then just to piggyback on some of the other questions, knowing that there were casualties associated with those detainees to Afghanistan, you then as an administration decided then it was okay to still release detainees to Afghanistan? Is that correct?

Mr. WOLOSKY. It may have been correct at the moment. I can assure you that each detainee transferred to Afghanistan or, frankly, anywhere else is subject to the review of the Chairman of the Joint Chiefs of Staff and I can tell you that the State Department would not concur in any transfer of a detainee to Afghanistan over the objection of the Chairman of the Joint Chiefs of Staff.

Mr. SALMON. Well, prior to releasing detainees to Afghanistan, did the intelligence community assess that the Government of Afghanistan was incapable of maintaining custody and control of these individuals?

Mr. WOLOSKY. The standard isn't maintaining custody and control because they are not transferred into custody. The standard is substantially mitigating the threat that they may pose and, again, these are determinations that would have been made in conjunction with and subject to the consultation with the Chairman of the Joint Chiefs of Staff if in fact they occurred in this administration. I believe that there have been.

Mr. LEWIS. Yes, Congressman, there have been transfers to Afghanistan and as Envoy Wolosky says, we do consult with the field commanders in Afghanistan prior to any transfer and, again, those transfers have been made under the statutory standard that any threat is going to be substantially mitigated by the host nation. So it is better to talk about this in a closed setting, sir.

Mr. SALMON. But you did state for the record that one of your criteria for releasing them to Afghanistan was not monitoring. That's not a concern. You didn't care whether they were able to monitor or not?

Mr. WOLOSKY. We can't speak to specific security assurances with specific countries in an open session. But what I can say is that any transfer to Afghanistan would have involved the consultation and concurrence of the Chairman of the Joint Chiefs of Staff.

That's certainly what we do in all transfers, particularly in a place like Afghanistan. We at the State Department currently would not consent to any transfer to a place like Afghanistan unless the Chairman of the Joint Chiefs of Staff concurs in the transfer.

Mr. SALMON. Well, Afghanistan is an active war zone and it is also one of the most corrupt countries in the world, and so I guess what a lot of us would like to better understand is if monitoring isn't part of the decision and making sure that their whereabouts are readily ascertained, I guess a lot of us wonder why that isn't one of the criteria.

Thank you, Mr. Chairman. Yield back.

Mr. ROHRABACHER. The Chair now recognizes Mr. Weber.

Mr. WEBER. Thank you, Mr. Chair.

Envoy Wolosky, is that how you're saying that?

Mr. WOLOSKY. Yes, sir.

Mr. WEBER. Okay. You said that the standard was not the elimination of risk but a mitigation of risk in your earlier comments. Was that true under the prior administration as well?

Mr. WOLOSKY. I don't believe so.

Mr. WEBER. So you all came in—the current administration came in with that in 2009, basically?

Mr. WOLOSKY. Actually, the Congress came in with that. It's written into the NDAA. It's a piece of legislation passed by the Congress and signed into law by President Obama.

Mr. WEBER. So that was the standard that you used? That's pretty shocking what Congressman Duncan revealed, that we were told that Uruguay was not going to be able to monitor these guys' travel. There were six terrorists and I am not knowledgeable or privy to who they were. These were not the five that was released in exchange for Bergdahl. Is that correct?

Mr. WOLOSKY. Correct.

Mr. WEBER. Is it fair to say that in the Bush administration didn't they attempt to try to release what was assessed to be the lower level risk combatants at first?

Mr. WOLOSKY. I can't speak to that. I don't know what their process was.

Mr. WEBER. Is it fair to say in the current administration, that you chose to release the lower risk first and held the worse to the last?

Mr. WOLOSKY. The worst we are not releasing. We're only releasing or transferring subject to security assurances those individuals who have been designated as approved for transfer by the six agencies and departments of the government that are responsible for those decisions.

Mr. WEBER. But common sense would probably dictate that the Bush administration followed those same guidelines?

Mr. WOLOSKY. I don't think that that is a fair assumption, respectfully. One reason why it is not a fair assumption is for years we haven't released Yemeni detainees who in many cases are low-level fighters, if that, because of the circumstances in Yemen.

So currently many of the detainees who remain in Guantanamo and who are approved for transfer are from Yemen and that could reflect more their nationality than their risk profile.

Mr. WEBER. That goes to the risk profile and I am sure, too. Now, the five that were exchanged for Bergdahl are they—any of those back on the battlefield?

Mr. WOLOSKY. No. I am just going to defer to my colleague from the DoD to speak to that transfer because it was an anomalous transfer, as you know, negotiated by the Department of Defense as a prisoner exchange.

Mr. WEBER. Okay.

Mr. WOLOSKY. I am confident he will say no when he turns around.

Mr. WEBER. All right. Well, his time has passed. I am going to move to the next question. So there are countries who take—who the administration negotiates with and we have a disagreement about whether or not they actually will monitor them or not.

What number of countries do we look at for transferring these combatants to? Is it 6, 8, 26? How many countries are involved?

Mr. WOLOSKY. We can get you the numbers but I believe we've transferred detainees in this administration to, what, 30 or 40 countries?

Mr. LEWIS. We've resettled to 30 and then 9 repatriations back to their own country.

Mr. WEBER. Okay. So 30 countries. Are you monitoring? Are you able to track? You talked about—earlier in your comments you spoke with career government officials in making those assessments and those determinations. Career government officials on the United States side or on the prospective country side or both?

Mr. WOLOSKY. I was referring to the U.S. side.

Mr. WEBER. U.S. side. Okay. So of those 30 countries where we are sending people whether or not they can monitor them effectively or not and you said you're getting feedback—we called it—I think it was information sharing. Is that in real time?

Mr. WOLOSKY. It can be.

Mr. WEBER. It can be. But is it?

Mr. WOLOSKY. In some circumstances that I am aware of it is in basically real time.

Mr. WEBER. Was it in real time on the guy from Uruguay that got loose?

Mr. WOLOSKY. We can discuss that in closed session. I would welcome the opportunity to do that today if you would like to, sir.

Mr. WEBER. Okay. Okay. Of those 30 countries are you able to track in real time and even in retrospect are you able to track and say okay, this country did a good job of keeping up with their combatants, this country didn't, this country was okay, this country was lousy? Is there a scale of rating those countries and their abilities?

Mr. WOLOSKY. I am not aware of a scale. Certainly, the case——

Mr. WEBER. So how do you know going forward in the future? If a country doesn't do a good job, how do you say well, we'll give that country another one or two or three? How do you determine that?

Mr. WOLOSKY. By their record.

Mr. WEBER. Well, that would be a scale, wouldn't it?

Mr. WOLOSKY. I don't think so. It would be specific to the performance of a particular country—their monitoring, their information sharing with the United States. If we are not satisfied with the results on a previous transfer we wouldn't transfer a new one to that same place.

Mr. WEBER. Okay. Well, that makes sense. And then of the discussion you had with Mr. Duncan and Mr. Issa, you talked about the—those released under the previous administration, Bush, and there was 530, I think, released, and how many is under the current administration?

Mr. LEWIS. 159.

Mr. WEBER. 159. So I don't think that you and Issa agreed on the fact that somehow Bush released the good ones and Obama released the bad ones. Is that a fair statement?

Mr. WOLOSKY. That's correct.

Mr. WEBER. Okay. Would you say they were roughly equal?

Mr. WOLOSKY. It's impossible to generalize. Each case is different.

Mr. WEBER. Well, that——

Mr. WOLOSKY. What I was trying to do was to push back against the suggestion that Bush released the easy ones and we only have the hard ones.

Mr. WEBER. Right. But it is safe to say without——

Mr. WOLOSKY. It is not an accurate characterization.

Mr. WEBER. Well, without the specifics you can't accurately know that. But in general, a reasonable person might make that kind of assumption?

Mr. WOLOSKY. We are all about talking about specifics, not generalizations.

Mr. WEBER. Okay. Fair enough.

Mr. WOLOSKY. That is why we are here. It is why we have requested the opportunity——

Mr. WEBER. Okay.

Mr. WOLOSKY [continuing]. To speak with you in closed session because, frankly, a lot of what is said——

Mr. WEBER. Okay. Well, I am running out of time.

Mr. WOLOSKY [continuing]. Including about Uruguay is just inaccurate and I am happy to tell you if you're interested in learning the facts about why some of what was said——

Mr. WEBER. Let me—let me—we'll come back to that, Mr. Wolosky.

Mr. WOLOSKY [continuing]. In this hearing was inaccurate.

Mr. WEBER. Mr. Wolosky, I am out of time.

Mr. WOLOSKY. I am happy to speak to it.

Mr. WEBER. Mr. Wolosky, I am out of time. Let me just say thank you for being forthright but we are on a time limit. I've got two quick questions.

Mr. LEWIS. Sir, can I make—can I make comment, though?

Mr. WEBER. Yes, sir. You may.

Mr. LEWIS. Thank you, Mr. Chairman. There are 29 detainees that are currently eligible for transfer who we believe we can transfer safely and responsibly if we get security assurances——

Mr. WEBER. Can I make a suggestion?

Mr. LEWIS. Yes, sir.

Mr. WEBER. Don't send them to Uruguay.

Mr. LEWIS. Sir, many of them are Yemenis. That's why they are there.

Mr. WEBER. Mr. Wolosky, back to you.

Mr. WOLOSKY. Thank you, sir.

Mr. WEBER. You're welcome. At the end of the Uruguay program, you mentioned earlier that the guy got 3—2 months——

Mr. ROHRABACHER [continuing]. Your last question.

Mr. WEBER. All right. Two months early. Tell, for the committee's sake, what would an additional 2 months have done, in your opinion? Would it have rehabilitated that combatant? What would that have done?

Mr. WOLOSKY. This individual, Diyab, frankly, was a problem from the moment he landed in Uruguay and I'll tell you that and be up front about it. His resettlement was difficult.

He did not seem to want to participate in the opportunities that were being afforded to him by the government.

Mr. WEBER. Should we have had snap back sanctions in place, to use another term bantered around?

Mr. WOLOSKY. We are not repopulating Guantanamo.

Mr. WEBER. Thank you. Mr. Chairman, I yield back.

Chairman ROYCE. We go to Mr. Joe Wilson of South Carolina.

Mr. WILSON. Thank you, Chairman Royce, and thank you for your leadership on this issue, and it is so important. I've had the opportunity to visit Guantanamo twice to see the personnel there, the professionalism of our military. And it is the place where terrorists should be.

In my home State of South Carolina, we've learned a lesson. There was one terrorist at the Navy brig in Charleston. He's had a consequence.

He's attracted more terrorists to come to the community and threaten attacks on the facility, putting schools at risk, neighborhoods in the immediate neighborhood at risk. It's utterly absurd the thought of bringing them to the United States in any way or releasing them, and it is interesting you say Yemen.

You release people to Yemen, which was supposed to be an example of great success by this administration of establishing a stable country and within days of releasing and pardoning terrorists the country collapsed.

And it would be interesting to know, what did happen to the persons who have been released to Yemen previously?

Mr. WOLOSKY. We do not release individuals to Yemen.

Mr. WILSON. Well, you had previously released before the collapse of the country. But there is a consistency here which is not good and the consistency is we have an administration that has dismissed ISIS as a JV—junior varsity.

These are the same people after the announcement of junior varsity they committed mass murder in Jakarta, in Brussels, in Paris, in Orlando, in San Bernardino. We know the mass murder, this week, in Baghdad and in Kabul.

Over and over again, there's been a dismissal of threats to American families. Additionally, it is incredible too this administration is very consistent by reaching a dangerous Iranian nuclear deal, providing tens of billions of dollars to a state sponsor of terrorism.

Just last week, the funding that has been provided by Iran to Hamas there have been rocket attacks on Sderot in Israel. Again, it is extraordinary to ignore this.

And then we come to pardoning and returning terrorists to go back on the battlefield. This is inconceivable and it is also quite illogical.

As you talk about a recruiting tool, a recruiting tool is releasing people—not being serious about detaining people who have every intent to kill American families.

And it is really interesting to me that they don't use the argument that it is a deterrent or it is a recruiting tool to have prisons within the United States. Of course, it is a deterrent.

If people know they are going to be incarcerated they are less likely to commit a crime or kill American families. And I am really grateful that even CNN yesterday reported that U.S. officials have said the 44-year-old Abu Wa'el Diyab, a Syrian national, went off the radar several weeks ago in Uruguay where he was resettled in 2014, not prior to 2009.

And so Uruguay's Interior Minister told CNN that Diyab was considered a refugee by the government and as such he would not need permission from Uruguayan authorities to leave the country.

They said he would only need permission from the foreign country he wished to enter per an agreement with U.S. that enabled the release of Gitmo detainees to Uruguay.

And there is a truth from CNN that I hope you look at and will reconsider that you are doing and that is that the disappearance could provide fuel for opponents of efforts to close the detention facility at Guantanamo, especially if Diyab is found to be attempting to join a terrorist group.

Of the 676 detainees released from the detention facility as of January, 118 have returned to the fight. An additional 86 are suspected of returning.

A recidivism rate of nearly one out of three released, according to a recent report from the administration's Office of Director of National Intelligence.

By releasing and pardoning these people, American families are at risk around the world and I just hope that you will reconsider what you're doing.

And then I am really grateful, in the Washington Post, Gordon England, the former Secretary of the Navy—and he's an extraordinary public servant. He is a person of the highest integrity.

He has warned that the process of releasing—the early process did work but that what's being done is that there were 200 detainees when he departed, none have been approved for release. Under the President, more than half have been released.

None of the low-risk, according to vigorous vetting, he has conducted during the Bush administration—statements by the country or the White House are misleading at best. And so I hope you will really reconsider and understand that we are in a global war on terrorism.

This is not an academic exercise of deterrence or incarceration, and I yield my time.

Chairman ROYCE. Okay. We go to Mr. Dana Rohrabacher of California.

Mr. ROHRABACHER. Thank you. Do any of you, either of you, know of cases—do you believe that Americans at Gitmo were involved with criminal mistreatment of the detainees?

Mr. WOLOSKY. I am not aware of that.

Mr. ROHRABACHER. Okay. So but the President has made it a national security imperative that we close Gitmo and this, we are told, that he has to close Gitmo because it has such a bad reputation. But yet from what you just said we know that those charges are not true. Is that right?

We have a propaganda campaign going on by the enemies of the United States and detractors of the United States against us, claiming that there was some kind of major criminal mistreatment of prisoners in Guantanamo and neither one of you know of an example of that or the fact is if there was one or two instances it certainly didn't reflect what was going on in Guantanamo, correct?

Mr. LEWIS. Sir, the issue is wrongfully so. There are many people around the world in many countries who think that there were things that went wrong at Gitmo.

Mr. ROHRABACHER. Right.

Mr. LEWIS. We don't believe that there were but they perceive that it happened.

Mr. ROHRABACHER. Well, let me correct it. Not only did a lot of people think that but there are people who hate our country who are promoting that knowing it is not true.

Let's get this in your mind. This isn't nice American politics. This isn't a criminal matter, although the President would like to think of these terrorists as being American criminals, Americans who have made a criminal act.

This is people who hate our way of life, they are engaged in an organized effort to terrorize Western civilization by murdering large numbers of noncombatants.

Mr. LEWIS. Sir, many of our——

Mr. ROHRABACHER. This is what we are trying to do. We are trying to handle this and what we get is a President who makes a national security imperative to give in to those people who propagandize and by doing that add some sort of credibility to whom?

To the charge that our people who are working in Guantanamo are a bunch of ghouls who are torturing these people. I totally— yeah, there may be one or two instances where somebody lost their temper or did something wrong.

But by and large, you know and we know that the prisoners in Guantanamo have been treated extraordinarily well. The President, by making it a national security imperative, has basically demonstrated that the propaganda, by people who hate us, will succeed and it will be seen and is seen as a sign of weakness by terrorists all over the world.

This very act that we are talking about is encouraging those people who will murder noncombatants, especially Americans. Let's get back to the number of 532 released by Bush.

Now, among those I know, for example, a lot of people were picked up. The Uighurs from Afghanistan had been picked up. They were in Afghanistan at the time of our operations. There were a lot of situations like that.

Obama has released 159. I think it is a bit disconcerting, again, when this administration insists on treating these terrorists and those involved in terrorist activities as nothing more than criminals.

You know, they are nothing more than like criminals would be in the United States. That's why, perhaps, the President finds it impossible to say the words ''radical Islamic terrorist'' because that is different than just some criminal who had committed an act of violence or murder in the United States.

And by doing so, again, seeing as a weakness, the President is actually encouraging terrorists around the world to take advantage of this weakness, take advantage of the fact we are willing to retreat if you just have a propaganda campaign.

I am glad to hear that we actually are suggesting that our guys didn't commit all sorts of horrible acts against these people. But of the 159 that were released—that have been released, what is disconcerting is when I hear that we don't have proof and it is been determined that this number of people have not—these people haven't committed any of these other acts after they've been released.

I, like Mr. Issa, find that totally—it is absurd, it is so bad. The fact is that we—if we are waiting for evidence to prove before we can say well, we think it is probable that they have been involved because we know what kind of people they are, that is one thing.

But what we are being told is unless we have overwhelming evidence that they have killed Americans or killed other innocent people, we are going to assume that they haven't.

Well, this is a way—this is not watching out for the security interests of the people of the United States. This is projecting weakness. This is going to make sure that more Americans die if by nothing else giving in and having the President of the United States insisting on treating terrorists as if they are American criminals, which will do nothing but encourage terrorism overseas. Thank you very much.

Chairman ROYCE. I thank the gentleman. We go to Mike McCaul, chairman of the Homeland Security Committee. Mike McCaul of Texas.

Mr. MCCAUL. Thank you, Mr. Chairman.

You know, the President campaigned on a promise to close Guantanamo. Is it fair to say that that campaign promise will not be fulfilled?

Mr. WOLOSKY. It's difficult to say. As you know, we are asking the Congress to reconsider its position on bringing a small number of detainees into the United States where, as you know, our Federal—as you know, better than most, Congressman, our Federal prison system has a 100-percent success rate in safely incarcerating over 400 convicted terrorists.

Mr. MCCAUL. So but the current plan is to process 29 transfers out of Gitmo, which would leave—I think there are 79 detainees. That would leave 50, I guess, at Guantanamo, right?

Mr. WOLOSKY. That's correct. You know, there are 10 that are in some phase of the military commission process and are being prosecuted or serving sentences.

The Periodic Review Board process is ongoing so it is possible that the number of detainees who were approved for transfer will increase. But your round numbers are generally correct.

Mr. MCCAUL. I've been down there. I saw Khalid Sheikh Mohammed, evil incarnate. So the 50 remaining—is it your intention to—we passed in the Congress under the National Defense Authorization bill an express prohibition against bringing these detainees into the United States.

This administration will honor that legal restraint, correct? It will follow the law.

Mr. WOLOSKY. As the President has said, his intention right now—his goal is to work with the Congress to change the law.

Mr. MCCAUL. Okay. What is the status of the trial of Khalid Sheikh Mohammed?

Mr. LEWIS. It's in the motions phase, sir.

Mr. MCCAUL. Why is this taking so long? I was a Federal prosecutor. This has been, you know, since 9/11.

Mr. LEWIS. Sir, I am a former Federal prosecutor as well. Other people are better placed to answer your question. But broadly, what I'll tell you is it is a new process so everything is new.

There's no precedent. There are a bunch of very good defense counsels and the judge is being careful and deliberative. We have a very good chief prosecutor, General Martins, who's trying very hard. But it is just, you know, the law—to do the law carefully, as you know, sir, is a careful process.

Mr. MCCAUL. Right. And I know defense counsel is filing a lot of motions. Pretty nice courtroom down there. There are 50 detainees that will be left. How many of those will be facing military trials?

Mr. LEWIS. Right now, as Envoy Wolosky said, there are seven that are in the motions phase. The 9/11 five, the alleged Cole bomber and then one more al-Qaeda leader. There are three in the sentencing phase, and we are continually looking at the others to see if there can be a case. But I am not in best place to tell you where we'd be.

Mr. MCCAUL. Getting back to those who you plan to release, we know 13 released have been implicated in attacks against the United States or coalition forces in Afghanistan, not a good number.

Let me ask you this question. Has the administration ever refused to send detainees to a country because it could not provide adequate security?

Mr. WOLOSKY. Absolutely. There are many countries that we look at that we ultimately determined are not suitable for this.

Mr. MCCAUL. You mentioned a lot of these detainees you want to transfer out are Yemenis. Yemen is a failed state, in my judgement, and it is in a really bad state of affairs.

You have the Houthis down there, Iranian forces. You have al-Qaeda in the Arabian Peninsula still plotting external operations against the United States. Can you tell me definitively you'll not be sending these detainees to Yemen?

Mr. WOLOSKY. Yes.

Mr. MCCAUL. Okay. That's a very good answer. What country would most likely receive them?

Mr. WOLOSKY. I'd prefer to talk to you in closed session about that. I mean, what I will say, as you know, generally we prefer repatriations to resettlements because of cultural affinities, language skills, family connections. In this case, you know, that is not going to be possible for Yemen. So we are looking at other alternatives.

Mr. MCCAUL. The last question—the Saudis have a pretty good deradicalization program. Have you considered that?

Mr. WOLOSKY. Yes. In fact, we transferred a number of Yemenis, I believe, nine to Saudi Arabia in April.

Mr. MCCAUL. Okay. I see my time has expired. Thank you.

Chairman ROYCE. Thank you. Thank you.

I want to get back to the issue of what you told this committee in March, just in closing here. We asked specific questions about the transfer of detainees to countries ill-equipped to handle them and specifically we asked whether the Department of Defense ever transferred a detainee to a country that it knew was incapable of maintaining control of that individual and keeping him from returning to the battlefield.

And Mr. Lewis responded no and Mr. Wolosky stated that he was not aware of such an instance. Your written response to the committee's letter, though, sent just this week states that the law doesn't prohibit us from sending detainees to countries that have partially derogatory intelligence assessments.

Now, partially derogatory in common terms means can't contain or at least are seriously challenged in containing those terrorists. So why didn't you cite the law instead of suggesting to the committee that detainees were not being transferred to countries that were incapable of maintaining control of them when it is so clear that they are?

That's the point I wanted to make. That is why this seemed to me like misleading the committee. And while I appreciate the witnesses' willingness to speak to us in a classified setting, which we'll take advantage of, that can't hide the fact that these issues can and have been discussed very productively here today.

As you can see, we have serious concerns about this policy and we'll continue the conversation.

But I do want to thank the witnesses and thank the members of the committee. The committee is adjourned.

Mr. ENGEL. Thank you, Mr. Chairman.

[Whereupon, at 12:06 p.m., the committee was adjourned.]

APPENDIX

MATERIAL SUBMITTED FOR THE RECORD

FULL COMMITTEE HEARING NOTICE
COMMITTEE ON FOREIGN AFFAIRS
U.S. HOUSE OF REPRESENTATIVES
WASHINGTON, DC 20515-6128

Edward R. Royce (R-CA), Chairman

July 7, 2016

TO: MEMBERS OF THE COMMITTEE ON FOREIGN AFFAIRS

You are respectfully requested to attend an OPEN hearing of the Committee on Foreign Affairs, to be held in Room 2172 of the Rayburn House Office Building (and available live on the Committee website at http://www.ForeignAffairs.house.gov):

DATE: Thursday, July 7, 2016

TIME: 10:00 a.m.

SUBJECT: Demanding Accountability: The Administration's Reckless Release of
                  Terrorists from Guantanamo

WITNESSES: Mr. Lee Wolosky
                  Special Envoy for Guantanamo Closure
                  U.S. Department of State

                  Mr. Paul M. Lewis
                  Special Envoy for Guantanamo Detention Closure
                  U.S. Department of Defense

By Direction of the Chairman

The Committee on Foreign Affairs seeks to make its facilities accessible to persons with disabilities. If you are in need of special accommodations, please call 202/225-5021 at least four business days in advance of the event, whenever practicable. Questions with regard to special accommodations in general (including availability of Committee materials in alternative formats and assistive listening devices) may be directed to the Committee.

COMMITTEE ON FOREIGN AFFAIRS
MINUTES OF FULL COMMITTEE HEARING

Day___*Thursday*___Date_____*7/7/2016*_____Room_____*2172*_____

Starting Time _____*10:18*_____Ending Time _____*12:06*_____

Recesses | *0* | (_____to _____) (_____to _____) (_____to _____) (_____to _____) (_____to _____) (_____to _____)

Presiding Member(s)

Chairman Edward R. Royce, Rep. Ileana Ros-Lehtinen, Rep. Dana Rohrabacher

---

Check all of the following that apply:

Open Session ☑   Electronically Recorded (taped) ☑
Executive (closed) Session ☐   Stenographic Record ☑
Televised ☑

TITLE OF HEARING:

Demanding Accoutability: The Administration's Reckless Release of Terrorists from Guantanamo

---

COMMITTEE MEMBERS PRESENT:

See attached.

NON-COMMITTEE MEMBERS PRESENT:

none

HEARING WITNESSES: Same as meeting notice attached? Yes ☑ No ☐
(If "no", please list below and include title, agency, department, or organization.)

STATEMENTS FOR THE RECORD: *(List any statements submitted for the record.)*

IFR - Rep. Eliot Engel
QFR - Chairman Edward Royce
QFR - Rep. Chris Smith

TIME SCHEDULED TO RECONVENE _____
or
TIME ADJOURNED *12:06*

_____
Full Committee Hearing Coordinator

HOUSE COMMITTEE ON FOREIGN AFFAIRS
FULL COMMITTEE HEARING

PRESENT	MEMBER
X	Edward R. Royce, CA
X	Christopher H. Smith, NJ
X	Ileana Ros-Lehtinen, FL
X	Dana Rohrabacher, CA
X	Steve Chabot, OH
X	Joe Wilson, SC
X	Michael T. McCaul, TX
X	Ted Poe, TX
X	Matt Salmon, AZ
X	Darrell Issa, CA
	Tom Marino, PA
X	Jeff Duncan, SC
X	Mo Brooks, AL
	Paul Cook, CA
X	Randy Weber, TX
	Scott Perry, PA
	Ron DeSantis, FL
	Mark Meadows, NC
	Ted Yoho, FL
	Curt Clawson, FL
	Scott DesJarlais, TN
	Reid Ribble, WI
	Dave Trott, MI
X	Lee Zeldin, NY
X	Dan Donovan, NY

PRESENT	MEMBER
X	Eliot L. Engel, NY
X	Brad Sherman, CA
	Gregory W. Meeks, NY
	Albio Sires, NJ
	Gerald E. Connolly, VA
	Theodore E. Deutch, FL
	Brian Higgins, NY
	Karen Bass, CA
	William Keating, MA
	David Cicilline, RI
	Alan Grayson, FL
	Ami Bera, CA
X	Alan S. Lowenthal, CA
	Grace Meng, NY
	Lois Frankel, FL
	Tulsi Gabbard, HI
	Joaquin Castro, TX
	Robin Kelly, IL
	Brendan Boyle, PA

OFFICE OF THE SECRETARY OF DEFENSE
WASHINGTON, DC 20301

The Honorable
Eliot L. Engel
U.S. House of Representatives
Washington, DC 20515

JUL 1 2 2016

Dear Mr. Engel:

I wish to ensure that the record is clear concerning my testimony offered at the Committee's July 7, 2016 hearing on detention operations at the United States Naval Station, Guantánamo Bay, Cuba. This letter provides clarification of an area of testimony in which the record does not clearly convey what I intended to communicate. I respectfully request that you accept this clarification in order to supplement and clarify the testimonial record.

At last Thursday's hearing, Representative Matt Salmon informed witnesses of his desire for specific information concerning former detainees who caused American deaths, and also concerning the Americans killed. He then referenced my previous testimony from March 23, offering that former Guantanamo detainees had caused American deaths. I responded to Representative Salmon that I understood that there were 14 detainees involved, and further stated that the intelligence community could provide the answers to all of his specific questions in this area. The relevant portion of the hearing transcript follows:

SALMON: Thank you Mr. Chairman. Last time you were here, Mr. Lewis you testified that Americans have been killed and I'm going to piggy-back on Mr. Royce and Mr. Duncan's questions. You subsequently notified the committee that those deaths occurred in Afghanistan by as many as 14 former detainees all who were released by the Bush administration and I'd just like to ask a few questions about that. How many Americans were killed? Were they U.S. servicemen and women, civilians or both? What are their names and where are they from?

LEWIS: Sir it's our understanding that there are 14, and I can get you the specifics on that. I believe we've -- the intelligence community can get you those specific details but the number is 14. Many of the incidents were large scale firefights in a warzone. So we can't always distinguish whether Americans were killed by former detainees or other participants, but the intelligence community can get you the specific details that you ask for sir.

Upon reviewing the transcript of last Thursday's hearing, however, it appears that when I responded, it could be interpreted that I was stating that 14 Americans were killed by former detainees. I was not making such a statement, and wish to ensure that the record is clear as to the true intent of my testimony; i.e., that I understand that 14 former detainees were involved in the deaths of an unspecified number of Americans. I did not intend to convey that 14 Americans were killed by former detainees.

I sincerely appreciate your dedication to continuing an honest dialogue in this matter as the Administration continues efforts to responsibly close the detention facility. I remain committed to working with your committee as we all endeavor to protect the United States and U.S. persons around the world.

Sincerely,

Paul M. Lewis

cc:
The Honorable Edward R. Royce
Chairman

MATERIAL SUBMITTED FOR THE RECORD BY THE HONORABLE ELIOT L. ENGEL, A
REPRESENTATIVE IN CONGRESS FROM THE STATE OF NEW YORK

March 1, 2016

Senator John McCain
Chairman
Senate Armed Services Committee
Russell Senate Building, Room 228
Washington, DC 20510

Representative Mac Thornberry
Chairman
House Armed Services Committee
2216 Rayburn House Office Bldg.
Washington, DC 20515

Senator Jack Reed
Ranking Member
Senate Armed Service Committee
Russell Senate Building, Room 228
Washington, DC 20510

Representative Adam Smith
Ranking Member
House Armed Services Committee
2216 Rayburn House Office Bldg.
Washington, DC 20515

Dear Chairmen and Ranking Members,

For over seven years we, a group of retired flag and general officers of the United States Armed Forces, have advocated the responsible closure of the detention facility at Guantanamo Bay. We have done this because it is what is best for our country. It is in our national security interests, and above all, it is about reestablishing who we are as a country.

Last week the administration presented its plan for closing the Guantanamo Bay detention facility. As the chairmen and ranking members of the House and Senate Armed Service Committees, yours is a solemn responsibility. We write to encourage you to use this plan as a foundation to come together and find a path to finally shutter the detention facility. This should not be a political issue. Former President George W. Bush determined that Guantanamo should be closed because, in his words, "…the detention facility had become a propaganda tool for our enemies and a distraction for our allies. I worked to find a way to close the prison without compromising security." The current plan similarly seeks to achieve that objective, following the advice of our nation's top military, intelligence, and law enforcement leaders.

Closing Guantanamo will not be easy, but it is the right thing to do, and we call on you to work together to accomplish it. We take heart that our nation has elected people who will exercise their conscientious judgment, but who will not allow politics to obscure courage. Compromise for the common good is the true exercise of leadership and courage.

Sincerely,

General Charles Krulak, USMC (Ret.)
Vice Admiral Richard H. Carmona, USPHS (Ret.)
Lieutenant General Robert G. Gard, Jr., USA (Ret.)
Lieutenant General Richard L. Kelly, USMC (Ret.)
Lieutenant General Charles Otstott, USA (Ret.)
Lieutenant General Keith J. Stalder, USMC (Ret.)
Major General Eugene Fox, USA (Ret.)
Rear Admiral John D. Hutson, JAGC, USN (Ret
Major General Michael R. Lehnert, USMC (Ret.)
Major General Eric T. Olson, USA (Ret.)
Major General Walter L. Stewart, Jr., USA (Ret.)
Major General Margaret Woodward, USAF (Ret.)
Brigadier General David M. Brahms, USMC (Ret.)
Brigadier General James P. Cullen, USA (Ret.)

General David M. Maddox, USA (Ret.)
Lieutenant General John Castellaw, USMC (Ret.)
Vice Admiral Lee F. Gunn, USN (Ret.)
Lieutenant General Claudia J. Kennedy, USA (Ret.)
Lieutenant General Norman R. Seip, USAF (Ret.)
Major General Paul D. Eaton, USA (Ret.)
Rear Admiral Don Guter, JAGC, USN (Ret.)
Major General Carl B. Jensen, USMC (Ret.)
Major General William L. Nash, USA (Ret.)
Major General Thomas J. Romig, USA (Ret.)
Major General Antonio M. Taguba, USA (Ret.)
Brigadier General John Adams, USA (Ret.)
Brigadier General Stephen A. Cheney, USMC (Ret.)
Brigadier General Evelyn P. Foote, USA (Ret.)

Brigadier General Alan K. Fry, USA (Ret.)

Brigadier General David R. Irvine, USA (Ret.)

Brigadier General Richard O'Meara, USA (Ret.)

Brigadier General Daniel P. Woodward, USAF (Ret.)

Brigadier General Leif H. Hendrickson, USMC (Ret.)

Brigadier General John H. Johns, USA (Ret.)

Brigadier General Murray G. Sagsveen, USA (Ret.)

Brigadier General Stephen N. Xenakis, USA (Ret.)

Questions for the Record Submitted to
Special Envoy Ambassador Lee Wolosky by
Representative Edward R. Royce
House Foreign Affairs Committee
July 7, 2016

Question:
Has the State Department ever made, or explored making, direct payments to any former GTMO detainee in conjunction with, or following, their transfer? If so, please provide relevant details regarding each instance.

Answer:
      The Department of State has not made direct payments to any former GTMO detainee in conjunction with, or following, his transfer. The Department of State is not exploring making such payments.

Questions for the Record Submitted to
Special Envoy Ambassador Lee Wolosky by
Representative Rep. Chris Smith
House Foreign Affairs Committee
July 7, 2016

Question:
In March 2016, a Uruguayan convert to Islam named Carlos Peralta stabbed David Fremd, a leader in the local Uruguayan Jewish community, while shouting *"Allahu Akbar!"* Do we know how Carlos Peralta was radicalized, and whether he had any contact with the Guantanamo detainees?

Answer:
The Department of State does not have knowledge of how Peralta was radicalized and does not know if he had any contact with former Guantanamo detainees.

www.ingramcontent.com/pod-product-compliance
Lightning Source LLC
Chambersburg PA
CBHW081748280526
45789CB00008B/2771